WANDA E. BRUNSTETTER's

Amish Friends

GATHERINGS

COOKBOOK

Over 200 Recipes for Carry-In Favorites with
Tips for Making the Most of the Occasion

SHILOH RUN ▲ PRESS
An Imprint of Barbour Publishing, Inc.

© 2019 by Wanda E. Brunstetter

ISBN 978-1-68322-866-0   33614081431032

All scripture quotations are taken from the King James Version of the Bible.

Cover photograph (top) by Doyle Yoder, dypinc.com

Interior photographs on pages 4, 6, 43, 63, 80, 193 by Richard Brunstetter

Published by Shiloh Run Press, an imprint of Barbour Publishing, Inc., 1810 Barbour Drive, Uhrichsville, OH 44683, www.shilohrunpress.com

Our mission is to inspire the world with the life-changing message of the Bible.

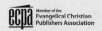
Member of the
Evangelical Christian
Publishers Association

Printed in China.

INTRODUCTION

My husband and I have attended many Amish functions, and most of them incorporated a tasty meal. Our Amish friends get together for many occasions that include weddings, biweekly church services, funerals, work frolics, ice cream suppers, young people singings, and charity events, as well as family gatherings such as birthdays, anniversaries, and holidays.

Most Amish gatherings involve sharing a meal or snacks with others in attendance. The meal following church is usually simple and light, such as bread, peanut butter spread, pickles, and cookies. However, meals on the day of an Amish wedding are more elaborate and filling, often including two or more kinds of meats, salads, condiments, and cooked vegetables. A special dessert at the end of the wedding meal is also served.

Amish gatherings aren't just about meals, however. They are a time for fellowship and bonding with others, whether it be simply working together or getting caught up on one another's lives. One of the things that make the Amish and other Plain groups unique is their desire to spend time with those in their community.

I hope you will enjoy the variety of recipes in this cookbook that are served at various Amish gatherings. A special thanks to my editor, Rebecca Germany, for compiling a good many of the recipes that were submitted by Amish friends.

Not forsaking the assembling of ourselves together, as the
manner of some is; but exhorting one another: and so
much the more, as ye see the day approaching.
HEBREWS 10:25

TABLE of CONTENTS

WHERE TWO ARE GATHERED

by Wanda E. Brunstetter

*For where two or three are gathered together in
my name, there am I in the midst of them.*
MATTHEW 18:20

A few years ago, my husband and I were in Ohio, where I was
scheduled to do some book signings. We were pleased when a
couple of our Amish friends from Pennsylvania hired a driver to bring
them to Ohio so we could spend a few days together. Even though
our time was short, the fellowship we had was sweet. We did some
shopping, shared a few meals, and attended church together. We told
stories from the past, talked about the future, and exchanged prayer
requests. Even though our Amish friends dress differently than we do
and live a different lifestyle, we have become close and enjoy each
other's company. We consider this couple to be among our dearest
friends and look forward to our times of fellowship with them.

God doesn't want us to close ourselves off from others. He wants
us to spend time with other believers and gather in His name. I always
feel the presence of God when I'm with a dear Christian friend. When
we share our joys, sorrows, and prayer requests with others, we feel
comforted and not alone.

*Where two or three are gathered
Fellowship is found.
The hum of gentle voices
Is such a pleasant sound.
Time spent with others
Is always a special treat.
Solitude can be lonely,
But fellowship is sweet.*
—WEB

Recipes for Beverages

Tea Concentrate

    4 quarts water
    1 quart tea leaves, packed
    2½ cups sugar

Bring water to boil. Add tea leaves to water and cover pot. Let stand 10 to 15 minutes. Remove tea leaves. Add sugar and stir until dissolved. Cool. Pour into 1-quart containers to freeze.

Mixing directions:

    1 quart frozen tea concentrate
    2 quarts water

Place in gallon pitcher. Allow tea concentrate to melt in water. Stir and serve.

Mary K. Bontrager, Middlebury, IN

COFFEE CONCENTRATE

Soak 1 large can of coffee (I use Folgers) in 6 quarts water. Let stand 24 hours. Strain out grounds. Store concentrate in refrigerator or freezer. Yield: 4 quarts.

FOR 1 CUP: 2 tablespoons concentrate and enough water to fill cup. Heat in saucepan.

FOR 100-CUP COFFEEMAKER OR 20-QUART CANNER: 2 quarts concentrate plus $4\frac{1}{2}$ gallons water. Heat to 190 degrees.

This concentrate is very handy to have on hand for church or other large gatherings. Can be frozen in small containers for home use.

Elizabeth Shetler, Brinkhaven, OH

ICED COFFEE

4 tablespoons instant coffee
1¼ cups sugar
3 cups hot water

ice
4 tablespoons vanilla
7 cups milk

In gallon pitcher, dissolve instant coffee and sugar in hot water. Add some ice to cool the mixture. Add vanilla and milk. Add lots of ice plus some more milk until pitcher is full.

Very good and refreshing on a hot summer day.

Miriam Raber, Flat Rock, IL

CREAM SAVER PUNCH

1 cup sugar
3 cups water
1 (12 ounce) can frozen orange
  juice concentrate
1 (64 ounce) can pineapple
  juice

1 (64 ounce) can V8 Tropical
  Blend juice
¼ cup lemon juice
1 (2 liter) bottle lemon-lime
  soda
Orange-vanilla sherbet

Boil sugar and water. Cool. Mix with juices. Freeze in containers. Move frozen containers to refrigerator 6 to 8 hours before serving. At serving time, place frozen mixture in punch bowl and add lemon-lime soda. To serve, put 1 scoop sherbet into goblets and fill with punch.

Judith Miller, Fredericktown, OH

FROZEN PEAR SLUSH

18 cups water
9 cups cane sugar

18 ounces (6⅓ cups) pineapple
  gelatin
36 cups chopped fresh pear

Boil water and sugar. Cool for 10 minutes. Add gelatin and stir until dissolved. Add chopped pears. Put into 8-ounce containers and freeze. Thaw 5 minutes before serving as a treat on a warm summer day.

Linda Burkholder, Fresno, OH

ORANGE DRINK

3 jars orange drink mix
10 gallons cold water
1 (2 liter) bottle orange soda

In 10-gallon milk can, dissolve drink mix in water. Before serving, add orange soda. Yield: approximately 100 servings.

We prepare this for the servers and cooks at a wedding to enjoy during the evening of singing.

Irene Hershberger, McKenzie, TN

Raspberry Slushy Drinks

2 cups water
2 (3 ounce) boxes raspberry
  gelatin
½ cup sugar
6 cups ice water

1 (46 ounce) can pineapple
  juice
1 (2 liter) bottle lemon-lime
  soda, chilled

Boil water. Add gelatin and sugar. Stir to dissolve, then add ice water and pineapple juice. Pour into larger container and freeze overnight. Set out about 2 hours before serving. Scoop slushy mixture into tall glasses, filling about ⅔ full. Finish filling with soda. Serve with straws.

Kathryn Troyer, Rutherford, TN

Strawberry Banana Slush

¾ cup sugar
2 cups water
6 ounces frozen lemonade slush

9 ounces water
2½ cups crushed strawberries
8 bananas, halved and thinly sliced

Heat sugar and 2 cups water; stir until sugar is dissolved. Stir in remaining ingredients. Spoon into small containers and freeze. Allow to thaw to a slush before serving.

Kari Danette Petersheim, Fredericktown, OH

Summertime Punch

10 lemons
10 limes
10 oranges

5 gallons water
10 cups sugar

Cut lemons, limes, and oranges in half and juice. Add juice to water. Stir in sugar until dissolved. Add ice to your liking.

We had this at our neighbor's wedding.

Mary K. Bontrager, Middlebury, IN

Rock-a-Bye-Baby Punch

3 quarts raspberry sherbet
6 liters ginger ale, chilled

Just before serving, put sherbet in punch bowl. Add ginger ale, stir until sherbet is almost melted.

Erma Yoder, Middlefield, OH

Wedding Punch 1

8½ cups sugar
12½ cups water
2 large cans orange juice
1 large can pineapple juice

2 small cans frozen orange juice concentrate
2 small cans frozen lemonade concentrate
2 (2 liter) bottles ginger ale

Mix sugar and water. Add juices. Chill. Add ginger ale just before serving.

Judith Miller, Fredericktown, OH

Wedding Punch 2

1 package cherry Kool-Aid
1 package strawberry Kool-Aid
2 cups sugar
3 quarts water

1 (6 ounce) can frozen orange juice concentrate
1 (6 ounce) can frozen lemonade concentrate
1 quart ginger ale

Mix all but ginger ale. When ready to serve, add ginger ale.

Irene Mast, Kalona, IA

GATHERINGS AMONG THE AMISH

by Amish friend Doretta Yoder, Topeka, IN

T he air is filled with sounds of greetings, laughter, and children's squeals. The driveway is full of black buggies as another Amish gathering gets underway.

It is typical for an Amish gathering to have a large attendance, in part due to the average size of an Amish family. I am Amish and was born into a family of six children, which is not considered unusual. I enjoy the three children I have been blessed with.

Food plays an important part of most any type of gathering—church, holiday celebrations, family reunions, church picnics, and work frolics, to name a few. Most times family, friends, or neighbors will offer to bring part of the meal, which is helpful. It would seem overwhelming to tackle it all by yourself, especially when you are cooking for large numbers.

For transporting food, I have all sorts of quilted warmers, thermal totes, baskets, and bags to choose from to wrap that special dish just right! Some Amish women sew custom covers for the roasters and pans we use a lot. To me it is very important to serve a hot dish hot and a cold dish cold! When done right, the potatoes can still be steaming when uncovered.

There are many recipes that I use in my cooking that have been passed down to me from my mom or grandma. Grandma makes the best meatballs! Nobody can make dressing like my mom! However, I am always discovering new recipes that are a hit at our gatherings.

Some ingredients that are common for me to buy would have seemed unnecessary to spend money on years ago. I guess time brings changes. I enjoy hearing the stories of getting up early and butchering the chickens for that day's threshing meal. It sounds like a lot of work, but can you imagine the freshness? With the invention of the freezer, we now work ahead. The majority of Amish buy their chicken from the butcher shop.

Many things have changed from when my grandma was young, but one thing remains the same: family traditions are still important! Gatherings might not be structured the same from community to community, but they are treasured just the same.

RECIPES FOR SNACKS

TIPS FOR PICNICS

* If you are eating outside, lay tea leaves around on the tables and between food dishes to keep the flies away.

* When you are having a cookout or picnic and don't have tablecloth clips, take wide-mouth canning jar flat lids and bend about 1½ inches from each side so it looks like a D. Slide over side of table over the cloth.

Mary K. Bontrager, Middlebury, IN

The Great Outdoors

We enjoy sitting around a campfire with friends and family, relaxing in the great outdoors, listening to God's creatures and the sounds of nature, and sharing stories while having s'mores, coffee, and tea.

Emma Jo Hochstetler, Nappanee, IN

Cheese Ball

2 (8 ounce) packages cream cheese
1 (8 ounce) package bacon cheese spread
2 tablespoons Worcestershire sauce
2 tablespoons onion flakes
1 (3 ounce) package dried beef, diced
½ teaspoon seasoned salt
Shredded cheddar cheese
Chopped nuts

Beat together all but nuts. Form into ball and roll in nuts. Refrigerate. Serve with crackers.

Susanna Mast, Kalona, IA

Cheesy Hamburger Dip

1 box Velveeta cheese
1 pound ground beef
1 envelope taco seasoning
16 ounces salsa

Melt cheese in slow cooker or glass casserole dish in oven. Stir often until melted. Meanwhile, fry ground beef and drain grease. Add taco seasoning. Mix beef and salsa into melted cheese. Bake at 350 degrees for 12 to 15 minutes until hot. Serve with chips or crackers.

Mary K. Bontrager, Middlebury, IN

Warm Bacon Dip

1 (8 ounce) package cream
   cheese, softened
1½ cups sour cream
2 cups (8 ounces) shredded
   cheddar cheese

1½ teaspoons Worcestershire
   sauce
¾ pound bacon, fried and
   crumbled
¼ cup chopped onion

In mixing bowl, beat cream cheese. Add sour cream, shredded cheese, and Worcestershire sauce; mix well. Stir in bacon and onion. Transfer to 1-quart baking dish. Bake uncovered at 375 degrees for 30 minutes. May garnish with additional bacon and cheese. Serve with crackers or chips.

Joann Miller, Mount Vernon, OH

Pizza Dip

1 (8 ounce) package cream
   cheese
½ cup sour cream
1 teaspoon oregano
⅛ teaspoon garlic powder
⅛ teaspoon red pepper flakes

½ cup pizza sauce
½ cup chopped pepperoni
½ cup chopped onion
½ cup chopped green pepper
½ cup shredded mozzarella
   cheese

Mix together cream cheese, sour cream, and spices. Spread in bottom of 9-inch pan. Layer on pizza sauce, pepperoni, onion, and green pepper. Bake at 350 degrees for 10 minutes. Top with cheese and bake another 5 minutes. Serve warm with crackers or chips.

Laura Miller, Mount Vernon, OH

BBQ Ranch Chicken Dip

1 (8 ounce) package cream
  cheese, softened
¼ cup barbecue sauce
6 ounces grilled chicken
  breast, chopped

¼ cup chopped red pepper
¼ cup sliced green onion
2 to 4 tablespoons ranch
  dressing

Spread cream cheese onto bottom of 9-inch pie pan. Spread barbecue sauce on top. Cover with chicken. Bake at 350 degrees for 10 to 15 minutes or until heated through. Top with peppers and onions. Drizzle with ranch dressing. Serve with crackers.

Jolene Bontrager, Topeka, IN

REFRIED BEAN DIP

1 can refried beans
1 pound ground beef, fried
1½ cups sour cream
1 (8 ounce) package cream
  cheese

2½ tablespoons taco
  seasoning
¼ teaspoon garlic powder
2 cups shredded Colby Jack
  cheese

Mix beans and beef; spread in 9x13-inch pan. Mix sour cream, cream cheese, taco seasoning, and garlic powder. Spread over bean mixture. Top with cheese. Bake at 350 degrees for 15 minutes until cheese is melted. Serve with chips or crackers.

Mary K. Bontrager, Middlebury, IN

PARTY MIX

1 box Honeycomb cereal
1 box Rice Chex cereal
1 box Corn Chex cereal
1 box Club cracker sticks
1 box Cheese crackers
1 box Wheat Thins crackers
2 bags Bugles snacks

1 bag Butter Snap pretzels
1 bag stick pretzels
2 pounds butter
1 cup vegetable oil
5 tablespoons Worcestershire sauce
2 tablespoons onion salt
2 tablespoons onion powder

Combine cereals, crackers, and snacks in large roasters. In large saucepan, melt butter, oil, and seasoning together, then pour over snacks. Mix well. Bake at 250 degrees for 1 to 2 hours. Stir every 15 minutes.

LeAnna Lehman, Sarasota, FL

RANCH PARTY MIX

1 cup oil
1 package ranch dip mix
1 round tablespoon sour cream and onion powder

2 pounds snack mix of choice, such as a mix of pretzels, Bugles, crackers, peanuts, Corn Chex, Kix, Honeycomb, and/or other

Mix together first 3 ingredients. Add snack mix. Mix well, then bake at 250 degrees for 1 hour in cake pan; stirring every 15 minutes.

Doris Schlabach, Goshen, IN

Sweet Cheddar Popcorn

1 cup popcorn kernels
Salt
¾ cup oil, warmed

½ cup sugar
½ cup cheddar cheese powder

Pop the popcorn, sprinkle with salt, and set aside. In mixing bowl, mix oil, sugar, and cheddar cheese powder. Pour over popcorn and bake in large pan at 300 degrees for 20 minutes, stirring every 5 minutes.

Jolene Bontrager, Topeka, IN

Roasted and Salted Pecans

7 cups pecan halves
5 tablespoons melted butter
2 teaspoons salt
Dash sugar

Mix all together. Spread on cookie sheet. Bake at 250 degrees for 1 hour, stirring every 15 minutes. Cool. Store in airtight container.

This is a good snack to take on trips or to give away as hostess gifts. For a bake sale, fill small cellophane bags and tie with ribbon.

Kathryn Troyer, Rutherford, TN

Fiber Balls

1 cup peanut butter
½ cup honey
½ cup ground flaxseed

¾ cup quick oats
1 cup shredded coconut
1 cup chocolate chips

Mix together. Roll into balls.

Rosanna Petersheim, Mifflin, PA

Energy Bites

2 cups oats
¾ cup ground flaxseed
¾ cup mini chocolate chips
2 tablespoons chia seeds

½ cup honey
1¼ cups creamy peanut
 butter
2 teaspoons vanilla

In large bowl, combine oats, flaxseed, chocolate chips, and chia seeds. Add honey, peanut butter, and vanilla. Stir until mixture comes together. Form into 1-inch balls and chill until firm. Yield: about 30 balls.

Diana Miller, Fredericktown, OH

Tortilla Rolls

8 ounces sour cream
1 (8 ounce) package cream cheese
1 (4 ounce) can diced green chilies
½ cup shredded cheddar cheese
½ cup chopped onion
1 envelope ranch dressing mix
⅛ teaspoon salt
⅛ teaspoon seasoned salt
½ diced ham
10 tortillas

Mix all together and spread onto tortillas. Roll each up. Secure and chill. Slice before serving. You may choose to add additional diced vegetables like broccoli and carrots.

There are never any leftovers when these are served.

Mrs. Mae Mast, Holmesville, OH

PRECIOUS MEMORIES

by Amish friend Lydiann Yoder, Andover, OH

My dad's family made many cherished memories by celebrating family members' birthdays. These were always evenings we looked forward to and were enjoyed by all.

My dad's birthday was in March. We would not tell him which evening everyone was coming so he'd be surprised. But his family's special efforts in cleaning up the house would always make him suspicious. The relatives would arrive with their families and freezers of homemade ice cream and toppings. A beautifully decorated cake made by Uncle Lester's wife would be admired by all. The cakes were made in various shapes and designs.

Soon the evening was over and the ice cream eaten. But we could look forward to Grandpa's birthday in June. Strawberries would be ripe by then and included in the menu. My uncles would tease me because I never wanted my strawberries on top of my ice cream but in a separate bowl.

Grandmother, two uncles, and two aunts had birthdays in September. They were all celebrated the same evening, usually at my grandparents' house. Again came the many freezers of ice cream with ice put in a gunnysack and chopped up. The ice man would bring ice twice a week.

Our uncle who lived closer to town would sometimes bring store-bought ice cream. We always chose the homemade first, though.

Since no strawberries were in season then and we had no freezers to keep any, we'd have chocolate dip to put on our ice cream instead. It was so yummy, especially when it was still warm and poured over the ice cream. I have included the recipe (page 192).

Time has a way of slipping by. We are now making memories for our families. Let's not be too busy to make family members' birthdays special by sharing it with them.

Recipes for
Breads and Rolls

Apple Bread

3 cups flour
2 teaspoons cinnamon
½ teaspoon baking powder
½ teaspoon salt
2 cups sugar
1 teaspoon baking soda

1 cup oil
4 large eggs
½ teaspoon vanilla
2 cups finely chopped apples
1 cup chopped nuts

Sift together flour, cinnamon, baking powder, salt, sugar, and baking soda. In mixing bowl, blend oil, eggs, and vanilla. Add flour mixture, stirring until just moistened. Batter will be thick. Fold in apples and nuts. Line two 4x8-inch bread pans with parchment paper and grease or spray with oil. Bake at 350 degrees for 50 to 55 minutes until toothpick inserted in middle comes out clean. Cool in pan 10 minutes before removing.

This can be frozen, wrapped in foil, and placed in a plastic bag. Great gift to give along with a jar of homemade apple butter.

Velma Schrock, Goshen, IN

MELT-IN-YOUR-MOUTH BISCUITS

2 cups flour
2 teaspoons baking powder
½ teaspoon cream of tartar
½ teaspoon salt
2 tablespoons sugar
½ cup shortening
1 egg
⅔ cup milk

Sift dry ingredients. Cut in shortening. Add egg. Slowly add milk to form sticky dough. Form dough into loose balls. Bake on cookie sheet at 450 degrees for 10 to 15 minutes.

Vera Mast, Kalona, IA

SOUR CREAM BISCUITS

3 tubes biscuits
1 tablespoon brown sugar
1 teaspoon cinnamon
½ cup melted butter

Quarter biscuit dough and place in greased 9x13-inch pan. Mix together brown sugar and cinnamon and sprinkle over top of dough. Pour melted butter over all. Bake at 375 degrees for 20 minutes. Spread icing over top while still hot. Best served warm.

ICING:

½ cup softened butter
½ cup brown sugar
1 cup sour cream

Mix well.

Mary K. Bontrager, Middlebury, IN

BREADSTICKS

1 tablespoon oil
2 cups water
1½ teaspoons salt

2 tablespoons sugar
1 tablespoon yeast
4 cups flour

TOPPINGS:

½ cup butter, melted
1 teaspoon garlic powder
2 teaspoons parsley flakes

3 tablespoons Parmesan cheese
1 teaspoon Italian seasoning

Mix dough ingredients well. Spread over greased cookie sheet and let rise 20 to 30 minutes. Add toppings and let rise an additional 20 minutes. Bake at 350 degrees for 15 to 20 minutes. When done, cut into sticks.

Diana Miller, Fredericktown, OH

QUICK BUTTERMILK ROLLS

¼ teaspoon baking soda
¼ cup sugar
½ teaspoon salt
1 tablespoon yeast

2½ cups flour, divided
1 cup buttermilk
3 tablespoons oil

Mix together baking soda, sugar, salt, yeast, and 1 cup flour. Heat buttermilk and oil until just below boiling or until small bubbles appear around edge of pan. Let milk mixture cool slightly. Add milk to flour mixture and beat well. Stir in remaining flour and knead dough until smooth and elastic, using more flour if needed. Roll out dough to about ½-inch thickness and cut into rounds. Place in two 8-inch round pans. Let rise until doubled in size. Bake at 350 degrees for 10 to 12 minutes or until lightly browned.

Esther L. Miller, Fredericktown, OH

Butterhorn Rolls

1 package yeast
1 tablespoon sugar
3 eggs
1 cup warm water

½ cup sugar
½ cup shortening
½ teaspoon salt
5 cups flour

Mix together yeast and 1 tablespoon sugar. Beat eggs with warm water. Let stand 15 minutes. Add ½ cup sugar, shortening, salt, and flour. Knead well. Let stand in refrigerator overnight. Next morning, divide into 2 parts. Roll out like piecrust in 12-inch circles. With pizza cutter, cut into 16 wedges. Roll up starting with wide end. Let rise 3 to 4 hours. Bake at 400 degrees for 15 minutes or until nice and brown. Brush with butter. Serve while warm. Can be frozen for later use.

Iva Yoder, Goshen, IN

Cinnamon Love Knots

2 tablespoons yeast
½ cup warm water
½ cup warm milk
½ cup butter, softened
½ cup sugar

2 eggs, beaten
4½ to 5 cups flour
2 cups sugar
2 tablespoons cinnamon
¾ cup butter, melted

Dissolve yeast in warm water. Let stand 5 minutes. Add milk, ½ cup butter, ½ cup sugar, and eggs. Stir in enough flour for a stiff dough. Turn onto floured surface; knead until smooth and elastic. Place in greased bowl. Cover and let rise until doubled, about 1 to 1½ hours. Punch dough down. Divide into 3 balls. Shape each ball into 12 balls, then roll each smaller ball into 8-inch ropes. Combine 2 cups sugar with cinnamon. Dip each rope in butter, then coat in cinnamon-sugar. Tie ropes into knots and place on cookie sheet. Let knots rise. Bake at 375 degrees for 12 to 14 minutes. Yield: 3 dozen.

Katie Schmidt, Carlisle, KY

Sandwich Rolls

1 tablespoon yeast	1 cup milk, scalded
½ cup warm water	⅓ cup sugar
1 tablespoon sugar	⅛ teaspoon salt
1 teaspoon baking powder	2 eggs
⅓ cup butter, melted	4½ cups flour

Dissolve yeast in warm water. Add 1 tablespoon sugar and baking powder. Let stand 20 minutes. Mix butter, milk, ⅓ cup sugar, and salt. Cool. Add eggs. Mix all ingredients together, adding flour last. Divide dough in half. Flatten onto 2 cookie sheets. Prick dough with a fork like you would for piecrust. Cut both sheets into 6 pieces. (I cut lengthwise then in half and 4 crosswise. Buns are approximately 4.5x9 inches.) Bake at 425 degrees for 10 to 12 minutes until lightly golden. Fold each piece in half while still warm. After they've cooled, fill each sandwich.

Katie Miller, Arthur, IL

Sticky Buns

¼ cup butter	½ cup powdered sugar
1 cup brown sugar	2 tablespoons butter
2 tablespoons corn syrup	2 small tubes buttermilk
2 tablespoons water	biscuits
1 (8 ounce) package cream cheese	

Combine ¼ cup butter, brown sugar, corn syrup, and water in saucepan and heat until melted, stirring constantly. Pour into 9x13-inch pan. Cream together cream cheese, powdered sugar, and 2 tablespoons butter. Set aside. Flatten biscuits and put 1 tablespoon cream cheese filling on each. Fold side up and press together at top to seal filling inside. Lay on top of caramel sauce, fold side up. Bake at 350 degrees for 30 minutes until nicely browned.

This recipe is excellent for coffee breaks and tea parties.

Esta Hostetler, New Concord, OH

Skillet Corn Bread (Gluten-Free)

1 cup gluten-free flour mix
1 teaspoon xanthan gum
1 cup yellow cornmeal
4 teaspoons baking powder
¾ teaspoon salt
¼ cup cane sugar

3 eggs
1 cup milk
¼ cup butter, melted
½ cup frozen corn (optional)
½ cup shredded cheese (optional)

Mix dry ingredients together. Blend in remaining ingredients. Pour into greased cast iron skillet. Bake at 350 degrees for 30 to 40 minutes or until done.

Julia Troyer, Fredericksburg, OH

Cornmeal Dinner Rolls

⅓ cup cornmeal
½ cup sugar
2 teaspoons salt
½ cup butter
2 cups milk

1 tablespoon yeast
¼ cup warm water
2 eggs, beaten
5 to 6 cups flour

In saucepan, cook together cornmeal, sugar, salt, butter, and milk. Remove from heat and cool until lukewarm. Dissolve yeast in warm water; add eggs. Add yeast mixture to cornmeal mixture, stirring well. Add enough flour to form soft dough. Knead in bowl and cover. Let rise until double in size and punch down. Form into balls for dinner rolls or roll out to 1-inch thickness and cut with biscuit cutter. Place on greased cookie sheet. Let rise until almost double in size. Bake at 375 degrees for 15 minutes or until golden. Brush with butter.

We use this recipe for our wedding reception dinners. The cornmeal mixture gives them a soft texture and pretty golden color.

Phebe Peight, McVeytown, PA

PUMPKIN MUFFINS

1 cup sugar
3 eggs
1 cup oil
2 cups cooked pumpkin or
    sweet potato
5 cups flour

1½ teaspoons baking powder
1½ teaspoons baking soda
1½ teaspoons salt
1½ teaspoons cinnamon
½ teaspoon vanilla
¾ to 1 cup milk

Cream together sugar, eggs, oil, and pumpkin. Mix together remaining ingredients except milk. Add dry mixture alternately with milk to creamed mixture. Put in greased muffin tins. Bake at 400 degrees for 12 minutes. Batter will keep in refrigerator for up to 2 weeks.

Anna M. Byler, Clymer, PA

Best-Ever Cinnamon Rolls

6 cups flour
1 cup sugar
4 teaspoons salt
3 tablespoons yeast
1 cup lard
4 eggs

3 cups lukewarm milk
4 cups flour
2 cups brown sugar
4 teaspoons cinnamon
¼ cup melted butter
Heavy cream

In large mixing bowl, combine 6 cups flour, sugar, salt, and yeast. Add lard, eggs, and milk, mixing well until smooth and elastic. Gradually add 4 cups flour and knead until smooth. Do not grease bowl as you might for bread. Let dough rise, punch it down, and let rise again before rolling out dough into an oblong shape. In bowl, combine brown sugar, cinnamon, and butter and spread over dough. Roll up dough and cut into ¾-inch slices. Put slices into pan. Spoon 1 tablespoon of cream onto each roll. Let rise. Bake at 350 degrees for 20 minutes. Frost. I use a cream cheese icing.

VARIATION: To make fruit-filled rolls, omit the cinnamon-sugar-butter mixture. Roll and slice the dough. Spoon on the cream, then add a spoonful of pie filling of your choice (we like raspberry) to the center of each roll. Bake.

Verena N. Schwartz, Scottsburg, IN

Grandma Ella's Bread

2 cups warm water
1 tablespoon yeast
¼ cup brown sugar
¼ cup oil

1 teaspoon salt
2 cups whole wheat flour
3½ cups Tesco bread flour

Combine warm water and yeast; let stand until foamy. Add brown sugar, oil, and salt; mix well. Add whole wheat flour; mix well. Add remaining flour 1 cup at a time, kneading well. Cover and let rise until double in size—approximately 30 minutes. Knead and divide into thirds. Shape into loaves and put into well-oiled bread pans. Let rise until double, then bake at 325 degrees for 30 minutes.

A simple but good everyday bread.

Mrs. Alfred (Barbara) Stutzman, Danville, OH

Whole Wheat Bread

¾ cup coconut oil
½ cup maple syrup or honey
5¼ cups warm (115 degrees)
   water
14 to 15 cups flour (half
   Bronze Chief and half

Prairie Gold), divided
3 tablespoons yeast
4 eggs, beaten
1¼ teaspoons salt
3 tablespoons sunflower
   lecithin

Mix coconut oil and maple syrup in small saucepan and heat to 120 to 125 degrees. Combine heated mixture with warm water in large mixing bowl. Quickly whisk in 5 cups flour and beat until smooth. Add yeast and mix well. Mixture may appear slightly lumpy. Cover bowl and let rise in warm place for 25 minutes. Add eggs, salt, and lecithin to dough; stir well. Slowly fold in 8 cups flour using circular motion. Continue stirring until 1½ to 2 cups more flour are worked into dough. Knead for at least 15 minutes. Divide dough into 2 bowls and let rise 1 hour in warm place. Divide dough into 5 greased loaf pans and let rise again. Bake at 350 degrees for 30 minutes.

Verena N. Schwartz, Scottsburg, IN

Amish Work Frolics

by Wanda E. Brunstetter

The Amish show their love for others by helping out whenever there's a need. When a new house or barn is required, many Amish gather for a time of work, which also results in socializing. The Amish and other Plain communities do many other things that involve them in community service. Amish women will get together to make quilts and other items to be sold at various benefit auctions.

The Amish view work as helping others. Members reach out to those with a need, knowing someday they too might receive help if there is a hardship. Following a flood or fire, the Amish community rallies to clean up the debris or construct a new building. Sometimes they might travel outside their community to assist non-Amish families that are victims of natural disasters.

Parents gather to clean up local schools in preparation for each new school year. Families that are moving can expect many helpers to carry furniture. An injured farmer will often get his crops harvested by his Amish neighbors. Extended family members and neighbors get together to paint a newlywed couple's house. Several adult siblings may get together in a work frolic that could involve sewing, housecleaning, gardening, or canning fresh produce.

The old saying "Many hands make light work" is certainly true among the Amish. At work frolics and barn raisings, there's always more than enough help to get the job done. Even for things like preparing meals, cleaning the house, and doing outside chores, everyone chips in.

RECIPES FOR SALADS

TIPS FOR PLANNING AHEAD

When I'm expecting company, I like to prepare food ahead.

* Mix meat loaf or hamburger patties ahead. It can be stored in the refrigerator 2 to 3 days.

* Pork and beans made the day before and warmed in the oven before serving have a wonderful flavor.

* Salads can be prepared in early morning the day of the dinner.

* For pies, make crusts up to 2 weeks ahead, freeze, and thaw the day before filling and baking.

* Pie fillings can be prepared 2 days before filling crust and baking.

Susie Kinsinger, Fredericktown, OH

* To thaw meat last-minute for company or an unexpected event, put meat in cold water (not warm or hot). Cold water thaws faster and is better for the meat.

Mary K. Bontrager, Middlebury, IN

Melon Ambrosia

1 cup cubed or balled
  watermelon
1 cup cubed or balled
  cantaloupe
1 cup cubed or balled
  honeydew melon

⅓ cup lime juice
2 tablespoons sugar
2 tablespoons honey
Pineapple (optional)
Fresh mint (optional)

In bowl, combine melon. In small bowl, blend lime juice, sugar, and honey. Pour over melon and toss to coat. Cover and refrigerate for at least 1 hour. Garnish with pineapple or mint if desired.

Mary Ellen Wengerd, Campbellsville, KY

Picnic Fruit Mix

1 cup water
1 cup sugar

2 teaspoons frozen lemonade
  concentrate
Fruit of choice

Heat water and sugar until sugar dissolves. Stir in concentrate. Cool and store in refrigerator until ready to use. Cut fruit into cubes, balls, or chunks until you have 9 quarts of mixed fruit. Chill fruit, then just before serving, mix syrup with fruit.

This is an attractive and refreshing dessert for summertime picnics.

Kathryn Troyer, Rutherford, TN

Easy Fruit Salad

2 quarts canned peaches, chunked
2 quarts fruit cocktail
1 cup instant lemon pudding mix

Drain peaches and fruit cocktail, reserving juice. Mix pudding mix into juice. Add back into fruit.

So simple and refreshing.

Anna M. Byler, Clymer, PA

Blackberry Gelatin Salad

3 small boxes black
   raspberry gelatin
3 cups boiling water
2 cups cold water

1 quart blackberry pie filling
1 (8 ounce) package cream
   cheese, softened
1 (8 ounce) tub whipped
   topping

Dissolve gelatin in boiling water. Add cold water and let set until syrupy. Remove 2 cups of liquid and set aside. Add pie filling to remaining gelatin mixture and stir well. Pour into serving dish. Chill until set. Beat cream cheese and slowly add reserved gelatin mixture. Beat well. Fold in whipped topping. Spread over blackberry layer and chill several hours.

Anita Lorraine Petersheim, Fredericktown, OH

Buttermilk Gelatin Salad

2 (20 ounce) cans pears
1 (3 ounce) box lemon gelatin
1 (3 ounce) box pineapple
   gelatin

1 (3 ounce) box apricot gelatin
6 cups cultured buttermilk
2 (8 ounce) tubs whipped
   topping

In blender, blend pears with juice until very smooth and fine. Pour into saucepan, add gelatin. Stir well and bring to full boil. Remove from heat. Stir until gelatin is fully dissolved. Cool to room temperature. Whisk in buttermilk. Fold in whipped topping. Pour into large serving bowl. Refrigerate several hours uncovered, then cover tightly.

This is refreshing, creamy, and light.

Kathryn Troyer, Rutherford, TN

GRAPE SALAD

1 (8 ounce) package cream
  cheese
½ cup brown sugar

1 tablespoon vanilla
3 pounds seedless grapes
1½ cups cashew pieces

Soften cream cheese and mix with brown sugar and vanilla. Stir until smooth. It will be thick. Pour over grapes and mix well. Add nuts. Mix and serve.

Lizzie Miller, Andover, OH

COOL LIME SALAD

2 cups crushed pineapple
1½ cups lime gelatin

24 ounces cottage cheese
3 cups whipped topping

In 3-quart pot, bring pineapple to a boil. Remove from heat and add gelatin. Stir until dissolved. Cool. Stir in cottage cheese and whipped topping. Yield: 12 cups.

Emma Zook, Navarre, OH

ORANGE-PINEAPPLE SALAD

1 (8 ounce) tub whipped
  topping
24 ounces small curd cottage
  cheese
1 can mandarin oranges,
  drained

1 (16 ounce) can crushed
  pineapple, drained
1 (3 ounce) box orange gelatin

Combine whipped topping and cottage cheese; mix well. Mix in oranges and pineapple. Add gelatin and mix well. Refrigerate.

Esther Schwartz, Harrisville, PA

ORANGE GELATIN PRETZEL SALAD

2 cups crushed pretzels
1 tablespoon sugar
½ cup butter, melted
2 (3 ounce) boxes orange
  gelatin
2 cups boiling water
2 (8 ounce) cans crushed
  pineapple, drained

1 (11 ounce) can mandarin
  oranges, drained
1 (8 ounce) package cream
  cheese, softened
¾ cup sugar
2 cups whipped topping

Combine pretzels, 1 tablespoon sugar, and butter. Press into ungreased 9x13-inch pan. Bake at 350 degrees for 10 minutes. Cool. In large bowl, dissolve gelatin in boiling water. Add pineapple and oranges. Chill until partially set. In small bowl, beat cream cheese and ¾ cup sugar until smooth. Fold in whipped topping. Spread over crust. Gently spoon gelatin mixture over cream cheese layer. Cover and refrigerate until firm. Yield: 15 servings.

Jolene Bontrager, Topeka, IN

STRAWBERRY PRETZEL SALAD

3 tablespoons sugar
¾ cup margarine or butter
2⅔ cups crushed pretzels
1 (8 ounce) package cream
  cheese, softened
1 scant cup sugar

1 cup whipped topping
2 (3 ounce) boxes strawberry
  gelatin
2 cups boiling water
2 quarts frozen strawberries

Cream 3 tablespoons sugar with margarine. Add pretzels. Spread in 9x13-inch pan and bake at 350 degrees for 10 minutes. Cool. Mix cream cheese, 1 cup sugar, and whipped topping. Pour over cooled crust. Dissolve gelatin in boiling water. Add frozen strawberries. Cool. Pour over cream cheese layer.

Ada Mast, Kalona, IA

Frosted Orange Salad

1 cup orange gelatin
3 cups boiling water
2½ cups miniature
    marshmallows
3 cups cold water
1 cup crushed pineapple,
    drain and reserve juice
4 medium bananas

½ cup sugar
1 tablespoon flour
1 egg, beaten
1 cup whipping cream
1 (8 ounce) package cream
    cheese
Pecans, chopped
Coconut, shredded

In large bowl, dissolve gelatin in boiling water. Add marshmallows to dissolve them. Add cold water, pineapple, and bananas. Pour into large serving bowl. Chill until firm. In saucepan, combine sugar, flour, and pineapple juice until smooth. Cook for 2 minutes, stirring constantly. Stir in egg and cook 2 more minutes. Cool. In a mixing bowl, beat whipping cream to stiff peaks. Mix in cream cheese. Add cooled cooked mixture. Beat until stiff and spread over gelatin. Garnish with pecans and coconut.

Verna Stutzman, Navarre, OH

Bacon Chicken Salad

Dressing:

½ cup mayonnaise
5 tablespoons barbecue sauce
3 tablespoons chopped onion
½ teaspoon salt
1 tablespoon lemon juice
3 tablespoons sugar
¼ teaspoon pepper
¼ teaspoon liquid smoke

Mix together until well blended.

Salad:

4 cups chopped lettuce
4 cups chopped spinach
2 large tomatoes, diced
1½ pounds chicken nuggets, cooked and cubed
10 bacon strips, fried and chopped
2 hard-boiled eggs, chopped
Shredded cheese

Layer first 6 ingredients in order given. Drizzle with dressing and top with cheese.

Jolene Bontrager, Topeka, IN

BROCCOLI STRAWBERRY SALAD

8 cups broccoli florets
8 ounces Swiss cheese, cut in
  ½-inch cubes
2 cups sliced fresh
  strawberries
¼ cup sliced almonds,
  toasted

1 cup mayonnaise
2 tablespoons sugar
2 teaspoons apple cider
  vinegar

Combine broccoli, cheese, strawberries, and almonds. In small bowl, blend mayonnaise, sugar, and vinegar. Drizzle over salad and mix.

Jolene Bontrager, Topeka, IN

CARROT SALAD

1 (3 ounce) box lemon gelatin
3 (3 ounce) boxes orange
  gelatin
1 package orange Kool-Aid
3 cups boiling water
4½ cups cold water

¾ cup finely chopped celery
1 medium carrot, shredded
½ (20 ounce) can crushed
  pineapple with juice
½ cup + 2 tablespoons finely
  chopped pecans

Mix gelatin and Kool-Aid; add boiling water, stirring until dissolved. Add cold water and let congeal slightly. Add celery, carrot, and pineapple. Pour into 3-quart bowl. Sprinkle with pecans. Refrigerate overnight.

As a young girl growing up, when we had company and I wanted to make something, Mother sometimes said I could make this, though she never had a recipe. I finally created one.

Esther L. Miller, Fredericktown, OH

LAYERED COLESLAW

1 cup Miracle Whip salad
  dressing
¼ teaspoon salt
1½ teaspoons mustard
½ cup sugar
5 tablespoons milk
1 head cabbage, shredded
Cheddar cheese, shredded
Bacon, fried and crumbled
Tomatoes, cut in wedges

Blend salad dressing, salt, mustard, sugar, and milk. Coat cabbage with dressing. You may not need all the dressing to cover the cabbage well. You don't want it too wet. On a large serving platter, spread out cabbage. Top with cheese, bacon, then tomatoes. Refrigerate.

Phebe Peight, McVeytown, PA

CHEESEBURGER SALAD

¾ pound ground beef,
  browned
½ cup chopped dill pickles
¾ cup ketchup
1 tablespoon mustard
Lettuce
Tomatoes, chopped
Onion, chopped
Shredded cheese
Croutons

Mix together beef, pickles, ketchup, and mustard. Layer in bowl starting with lettuce, then beef mixture, tomatoes, onion, cheese, and croutons. Good served with Western dressing (page 62).

Jolene Bontrager, Topeka, IN

Corn Chip Salad

1 head lettuce, shredded
2 pounds Colby cheese, grated

1 bag Fritos corn chips, crushed
2 (15.5 ounce) cans red kidney beans, drained and rinsed

Combine ingredients. Just before serving, pour dressing over and mix in.

Dressing:

1 cup Miracle Whip
⅛ cup vinegar
½ teaspoon paprika
2 teaspoons water
¼ cup oil

¾ cup sugar
¼ cup ketchup
1 teaspoon mustard
¼ teaspoon salt

Blend ingredients together.

Laura Miller, Mount Vernon, OH

Pasta Salad

6 cups uncooked pasta	2 cups cubed ham
2 cups cubed yellow cheese	2 cups chopped tomatoes
2 cups cubed white cheese	1 cup chopped bell peppers

Cook pasta in water for 11 minutes. As soon as pasta is done cooking, dump in strainer and run cold water through until it's cold. This keeps pasta from becoming mushy. Add remaining ingredients to pasta when cooled.

Dressing:

1 cup sugar	¼ teaspoon salt
1⅓ cups Italian dressing	¼ teaspoon pepper
2 tablespoons vegetable oil	1 tablespoon parsley flakes

Mix ingredients well. Add enough to pasta to make it moist, but not too wet. This dressing can be kept in refrigerator for later use.

Mrs. Orley (Dianna) Yoder, Goshen, IN

CRUNCHY ASIAN SALAD

2 packages chicken-flavored
   ramen noodles
½ cup slivered almonds
2 tablespoons butter

1 large head cabbage,
   shredded
1½ cups diced grilled chicken
   breast

Crush noodles. Toast almonds and noodles in butter. Cool. Layer cabbage, chicken, and noodle-almond mixture in glass trifle bowl. Add dressing just before serving. Mix well.

DRESSING:

1 package Italian dressing
   mix
¼ cup vinegar
½ cup vegetable oil
2 tablespoons soy sauce

3 tablespoons water
½ cup sugar
¼ cup minced onion
1 package chicken seasoning
   from noodle package

Mix together until well blended.

Jolene Bontrager, Topeka, IN

MAKE-AHEAD LAYERED LETTUCE SALAD

1 head iceberg lettuce,
   chopped
1 head romaine lettuce,
   chopped
1 small head cauliflower,
   cut fine

½ pound radishes, sliced thin

Mix together and put in 9x13-inch pan.

TOPPING:

1½ cups mayonnaise
⅓ cup Parmesan cheese
¼ cup sugar

1½ cups shredded cheddar
   cheese
1 pound bacon, fried,
   drained, and crumbled

Combine mayonnaise, Parmesan cheese, and sugar. Spread over vegetables. Top with cheddar cheese and bacon. Refrigerate 24 hours or overnight before serving.

Kathryn Troyer, Rutherford, TN

Taco Salad

1 pound ground beef
1 large onion, chopped
1 envelope taco seasoning
1 medium head lettuce,
  chopped

8 ounces shredded cheddar
  cheese
1 cup chili beans, rinsed and
  drained
Diced tomatoes
1 bag Doritos chips, crushed

Brown ground beef with onion and taco seasoning. Cool. Toss together lettuce, cheese, beans, tomatoes, and beef mixture. When ready to serve, coat with Thousand Island dressing. Top with chips.

Thousand Island Dressing:

1 cup Miracle Whip salad
  dressing
½ cup sugar
¼ cup ketchup

¼ cup pickle relish
¼ teaspoon salt
Dash pepper

Combine and stir until well blended.

Mrs. Mae Mast, Holmesville, OH

White Taco Salad

1 head lettuce, cut up
4 cups cooked and chopped
  chicken
½ (2.5 ounce) can sliced black
  olives, drained

2 cups shredded mozzarella
  cheese
½ bag Ranch Doritos,
  crushed
1½ (16 ounce) bottles ranch
  dressing

Mix all together and serve.

Susanna Mast, Kalona, IA

Green Goddess Dressing

1 cup mayonnaise
½ cup sour cream
¼ cup chopped green pepper
¼ cup packed fresh parsley
   sprigs
3 anchovy fillets (optional)

2 tablespoons lemon juice
2 green onion tops, chopped
1 garlic clove, peeled
¼ teaspoon pepper
⅛ teaspoon Worcestershire
   sauce

Place all ingredients in blender; process until smooth. Store in refrigerator.

This delicious savory dressing has a beautiful green color.

Mary Joyce Petersheim, Fredericktown, OH

POPPY SEED DRESSING

¼ cup vinegar
⅓ cup vegetable oil
1 teaspoon onion salt
1½ cups sour cream

1 cup Miracle Whip
1 cup sugar
1 teaspoon salt
2 teaspoons poppy seeds

Blend all together in blender or with egg beater. Good served on tossed salads.

Jolene Bontrager, Topeka, IN

WESTERN DRESSING

2 cups Miracle Whip salad
  dressing
1½ cups sugar
¼ cup ketchup
½ cup vegetable oil

2 teaspoons mustard
1 teaspoon paprika
4 teaspoons water
½ teaspoon salt
¼ cup vinegar

Mix all together until blended. Very good on taco salad or cheeseburger salad.

Jolene Bontrager, Topeka, IN

Amish Schools

by *Wanda E. Brunstetter*

Amish children begin school in the first grade and end their schooling after eighth grade, at which time they learn some kind of trade. Although some Amish children attend public schools, most are taught in their own one-room schoolhouses. Normally just one teacher oversees all eight grades, but most teachers do have a helper. Some larger schools have two or three teachers.

A typical school day begins with a period of devotions, as a passage of scripture is read from the Bible. Following Bible reading, the children repeat the Lord's Prayer in unison. Next, they sing a few songs. Arithmetic is the first subject of the day; then comes spelling or English. Since Pennsylvania Dutch-speaking Amish children are taught the English language in the first grade, the teacher must give attention to them while the other children work on their own or with the assistance of the teacher's helper.

Amish parents are involved with the school in several ways. They not only take responsibility for being on the school board and hiring the teachers but also do the repairs and annual cleaning of the schoolhouses a few weeks before school begins each term. Most parents visit the school once or twice during the year, often dropping by without prior notice. Sometimes a hot lunch is brought to school by a parent, and various school programs are always well attended by the children's parents.

RECIPES FOR SIDE DISHES

TIPS FOR TRANSPORTING FOOD

❖ To keep food cold if you don't have ice packs, put a gallon-size zipper bag inside another bag of the same size. Fill inside bag with ice. Squeeze out air and seal both bags. Put inside your carrier before adding your cold dish.

Mary K. Bontrager, Middlebury, IN

❖ Save clean pizza boxes to transport pies, cookies, and rolls to bake sales, auctions, or other events.

Emma Jo Hochstetler, Nappanee, IN

❖ A good way to transport hot or cold food is to fold a bath towel so it fits in the bottom of an ice chest. Set your pot, roaster, or whatever is hot on the towel. Fold another towel and lay it on top and close the chest tightly. The hot food will stay hot! If you are taking a frozen dish, do the same with towels in an ice chest. You can also add dry ice packs. We've had it happen that the dish is still so frozen hard that it needs to sit awhile before it can be served.

Mattie Petersheim, Junction City, OH

❖ I like to use a clean bath towel or a clean blanket to wrap hot roasters in to keep the food from cooling.

❖ Wrap wet newspaper around ice cream containers. It may freeze on in places. Cover with more dry newspaper. The ice cream should not melt.

Anna M. Yoder, Mercer, MO

❖ Put your hot meat in an ice chest lined with aluminum foil. It will stay hot for hours.

Amanda Zehr, Spencerville, IN

BAKED MACARONI AND CHEESE

3 tablespoons butter	1 teaspoon salt
2½ cups uncooked macaroni	¼ teaspoon pepper
½ pound Velveeta cheese	1 quart milk

Melt butter in baking dish. Pour in macaroni and stir until coated. Slice cheese and layer on macaroni. Sprinkle salt and pepper over all. Add milk. Bake at 375 degrees for 1½ hours. Do not stir while baking. Fried sausage or browned ground beef is very good baked into this casserole.

Mrs. Albert (Ruth) Yoder, Stanwood, MI

Ozark Baked Beans

2 pounds ground beef, browned and drained

2 pounds bacon, chopped, fried, and drained (reserve grease)

4 (15 ounce) cans kidney beans, partially drained

4 (15 ounce) cans lima beans, partially drained

4 (15 ounce) cans pork & beans, partially drained

4 cups chopped onion

1⅓ cups sugar

1½ cups brown sugar

½ cup molasses

1 cup ketchup

1 cup barbecue sauce

¼ cup mustard

4 teaspoons chili powder

2 teaspoons salt

½ teaspoon pepper

Mix all together in roasting pan, adding some reserved bacon grease if desired. Bake at 350 degrees for 1 hour.

Mary Ellen Wengerd, Campbellsville, KY

SHANTY BEANS

1 pound dried lima beans
5 cups cold water
¾ pound sliced bacon

Salt and pepper to taste
¾ pound brown sugar

Soak lima beans in water overnight. Drain off water. Place beans in saucepan and just cover with fresh water. Cut bacon in 1-inch squares. Add to beans and cook. Add salt and pepper. Be sure you can see pepper after beans are stirred. When soft, take off heat and add brown sugar. Let stand a few minutes before serving.

Anna M. Byler, Clymer, PA

COPPER PENNIES

2 pounds carrots, peeled and
   sliced
1 green pepper, thinly sliced
1 large onion, thinly sliced
1 teaspoon salt
½ teaspoon pepper

¾ cup sugar
¼ cup vinegar
1 can tomato soup
½ cup salad oil
¼ teaspoon dry mustard

Cook carrots until barely tender, then cool. Layer vegetables in bowl and sprinkle with salt and pepper. Mix together sugar, vinegar, soup, oil, and dry mustard. Pour over vegetables. Cover and refrigerate 8 to 12 hours before serving. This can also be served hot. Bake at 325 degrees for 30 minutes.

Mrs. Elizabeth Miller, Middlefield, OH

BBQ Green Beans

½ pound bacon or ham
1 medium onion, chopped
2 quarts green beans, drained
  (or use fresh beans)

¾ cup brown sugar
½ cup ketchup
1 teaspoon liquid smoke
½ teaspoon salt

Fry bacon and onion. Drain. Add green beans. In saucepan, mix remaining ingredients and heat until brown sugar dissolves. Pour over beans. Bake at 325 degrees for 1 hour.

Jolene Bontrager, Topeka, IN

Cabbage Casserole

½ cup butter
1 head cabbage, chopped
2 to 3 cups sour cream

Salt and pepper to taste
2 boxes stuffing mix

Melt butter in large casserole dish. Layer cabbage on top. Spread sour cream over cabbage. Sprinkle with salt and pepper. According to stuffing mix box, add listed ingredients to stuffing mix, except for water. Put mixture on top of sour cream. Cover and bake at 350 degrees for approximately 45 minutes until cabbage is tender.

Lydia Miller, Loudonville, OH

Baked Corn

3 eggs
3 tablespoons butter
1 tablespoon sugar
1 tablespoon flour

1½ teaspoons salt
1⅓ cups milk, scalded
¼ cup onion, chopped
1½ to 2 cups corn

Put everything, except corn, into blender and process until well blended. Add corn and process only until corn is mixed into batter. Pour into 2-quart casserole dish. Bake at 350 degrees for 70 minutes.

This will transport well when wrapped in a towel.

Anna M. Byler, Clymer, PA

Beans and Mushroom Amandine

1 (16 ounce) can green beans
1 tablespoon finely chopped
  chives or green onion
2 tablespoons butter
3 teaspoons flour
¼ teaspoon salt

⅛ teaspoon pepper
¼ cup evaporated milk
1 (3 to 4 ounce) can
  mushrooms, drained
2 tablespoons sliced almonds,
  toasted

Drain green beans, reserving liquid. Cook chives in butter a few minutes. Add flour, salt, and pepper, stirring until smooth. Add milk and ¼ cup liquid from beans. Cook until thickened, stirring constantly. Add drained beans and mushrooms. Heat through. Serve sprinkled with almonds. Yield: 6 servings.

Judith Miller, Fredericktown, OH

Onion Blossoms

2 large sweet onions
1½ cups flour
1½ teaspoons oregano
1½ teaspoons pepper
1½ teaspoons salt

1½ teaspoons cumin
1½ teaspoons thyme
2 eggs
¾ cup milk

Cut up onions with blooming onion cutter or into onion rings. Put in cold water for a while. Mix dry ingredients; set aside. Mix eggs and milk; beat well. Heat oil to 350 to 375 degrees. Dip onions in egg mixture then in dry mix. Repeat. Fry until nice and golden. Place in warm oven until ready to serve. Sprinkle with Nature's seasoning if desired.

This is a good appetizer that everybody loves. I make extra because we like to eat them cold on salads or sandwiches.

Blossom Sauce:

1½ cups mayonnaise
2 tablespoons ketchup
2 tablespoons creamy
  horseradish sauce

1 tablespoon oregano
1 tablespoon pepper
1 cup Southwest ranch
  dressing

Mix all together. Make a couple of days before using so flavors can develop. Great for dipping anything!

Kathy Ebersol, Bristolville, OH

BAKED POTATO CASSEROLE

8 medium potatoes, peeled,
cooked, and cubed
4 tablespoons butter
1 cup sour cream

1 envelope ranch dressing
mix
2 cups shredded cheddar
cheese
Bacon, crumbled (optional)

Place potatoes in pan with butter. Mix sour cream with ranch dressing mix.
Spread over potatoes. Top with cheese and bacon. Bake covered at 350 degrees
for 60 minutes.

Esther M. Peachey, Flemingsburg, KY

SAUCE FOR BAKED POTATOES

1 cup sour cream
1 cup mayonnaise
1 teaspoon salt

$\frac{1}{8}$ to $\frac{1}{4}$ teaspoon creole
seasoning
$\frac{1}{4}$ teaspoon onion powder
$\frac{1}{2}$ teaspoon chives

Mix all together and serve on baked potatoes.

Kari Danette Petersheim, Fredericktown, OH

Campfire Potatoes

5 medium potatoes, thinly
  sliced
1 medium onion, sliced
6 tablespoons butter
⅓ cup shredded cheese

2 tablespoons minced parsley
1 tablespoon Worcestershire
  sauce
Salt and pepper to taste
⅓ cup chicken broth

Place potatoes and onion on pan that can be put in oven. Combine butter, cheese, parsley, Worcestershire sauce, and salt and pepper. Sprinkle over potatoes. Top with broth. Grill over medium-hot coals for 35 to 40 minutes.

Mrs. Levi J. Stutzman, West Salem, OH

Port-a-Pit Potatoes

1 cup butter
7 pints water
1 pint vinegar
1 cup brown sugar
¾ cup salt

2 tablespoons liquid smoke
2 teaspoons pepper
Small (1 inch) red potatoes
  with skins (or cut to 1-inch
  size)

Brown butter; add water, vinegar, brown sugar, salt, liquid smoke, and pepper. Bring to a boil. Add potatoes and cook until starting to soften. Turn off heat and let set for 1 to 1½ hours. Drain. Grill over heat to brown. Remember not to overcook potatoes. Serve with ranch dressing or ketchup.

Emma Jo Hochstetler, Nappanee, IN

Potluck Potatoes

5 cups milk
½ cup flour
1½ pounds Velveeta cheese, cubed
1 cup butter, melted
1 tablespoon chopped onion
1 pint sour cream
1 can cream of mushroom soup

2 cans cream of chicken soup
½ teaspoon pepper
1 tablespoon seasoned salt
1 tablespoon onion salt
½ cup sour cream and onion powder
6 to 7 pounds frozen shredded hash browns

In large saucepan, heat milk and flour to make a paste. Add cubed cheese. Stir until melted. Add remaining ingredients. Spread into large roaster. Bake at 350 degrees for 1 hour.

Mrs. Orie Detweiler, Inola, OK

BEST BROWN RICE

1 cup brown rice
1 teaspoon celery salt
1½ tablespoons chicken
  seasoning

¼ cup chopped onion
4 tablespoons butter, cubed
2½ cups boiling water

Mix all together in 2-quart casserole dish. Cover. Bake at 350 degrees for 1½ to 2 hours.

Velma Schrock, Goshen, IN

GRILLED RICE

1⅓ cups instant rice
⅓ cup chopped mushrooms
  (optional)
¼ cup chopped green pepper

¼ cup chopped onion
1 cup water
⅓ cup ketchup
1 tablespoon butter

Combine rice, mushrooms, green pepper, onion, water, and ketchup in 9-inch foil pie pan. Dot with butter. Cover with foil. Seal edges tightly. Put on hot grill for 14 to 15 minutes until liquid is absorbed. Fluff with fork. Also works with leftover cooked rice, just eliminate the water.

Mrs. Mae Mast, Holmesville, OH

VEGETABLE DISH

1 quart mixed vegetables
5 tablespoons mayonnaise
1 cup diced Velveeta cheese

1 sleeve saltine crackers,
  crushed
½ cup butter, melted
Taco seasoning

Coat vegetables with mayonnaise and place in 8x8-inch baking dish. Top with cheese. Combine cracker crumbs and butter. Spread over vegetables. Sprinkle with taco seasoning. Bake at 350 degrees for 30 minutes until golden.

Arlene K. Eicher, Carlisle, KY

Amish Dressing and Gravy

8 eggs	2 cups cubed toasted bread
1 quart milk	½ cup cubed cooked chicken
1½ teaspoons salt	½ cup cubed potatoes
1 teaspoon chicken base	½ cup diced celery
2 teaspoons parsley flakes	½ cup diced carrots

Beat eggs. Add milk, salt, chicken base, and parsley. Beat to blend. Add remaining ingredients. Fry as patties in skillet or bake in greased 2-quart dish at 350 degrees for 45 to 50 minutes. Serve with gravy.

Gravy:

¼ cup butter	Salt and pepper to taste
¾ cup flour	4 cups water or milk

In skillet, melt butter, then add flour and brown. Season. Add liquid 1 cup at a time. Stir constantly until gravy thickens.

This recipe is often enlarged and served for weddings. Amish housewives memorize this recipe. Often we can the last four ingredients with chicken broth and water to use as a quick starter base for making the dressing.

B. Saloma D. Yoder, Mercer, MO

Zucchini Dressing

1 stick margarine	3 eggs, beaten
2 cups coarsely grated zucchini	1½ cups cracker crumbs
½ cup chopped onion	½ cup shredded cheese

Melt margarine in large saucepan. Let cool 5 minutes. Stir in zucchini, onion, eggs, cracker crumbs, and cheese. Butter a 2-quart baking dish and bake uncovered at 350 degrees for 50 minutes.

Rosina Schwartz, Salem, IN

GOING TO CHURCH

by Amish friends Orley and Dianna Yoder, Goshen, IN

Our church services are most often held in a basement or shop building. During the summer months it is also not uncommon for services to be held in large tents, if the hosts do not have a basement or shop building big enough to hold the people. Backless benches are set up for up to 250 people. Services start at 9:00 a.m. and normally last until 11:30 or 12:00.

After the church service ends, a ten-to-fifteen-minute bustle occurs in preparing for lunch. The children leave the room and the elderly also get up from their seats but step to the side. The young to middle-aged men gather the songbooks together and put them away in specially made storage boxes. Then these men put together tables for lunch by placing specially made legs under the regular legs of the benches. Two benches side by side, on these legs, make a table. Usually four or five tables, each twelve-to-fourteen-feet long, are set up. After this is done, the women roll out the vinyl tablecloths and spread out the food, silverware, cups, and glasses over each table. Usually there is space for approximately ninety people to eat at a time. If there are more people than that, they eat in shifts. The women work together to quickly clean the tables, silverware, glasses, etc., for the next shift of hungry people.

The meal is generally considered a light lunch, the food being mostly bread with choices of spreads like peanut butter, jelly, and apple butter. Bowls of pickled cucumbers and beets are placed on the table. Ham and cheese are passed along once. Cookies are served as a dessert.

Four or five other ladies, usually neighbors or family members, each bake forty to fifty cookies, filling a good-size bowl, and bring them along to the church for the hosts to serve at lunchtime. Many different kinds are baked. People get a choice of cookie as they are passed along the table on a tray.

After all shifts of lunch are over, the ladies fix hot water in tubs and proceed to thoroughly wash the dishes before packing everything into boxes to store in the bench wagon. Each geographical church district of twenty to forty-five families has their own enclosed wagon that holds all the benches, dishes, and songbooks that are used for church, and this wagon goes from home to home.

As the ladies tend to the food and cleanup, they do their own chatting and socializing, while the men are off to the side, out of the way, visiting with each other. Serious conversations are held, but there are often some lighthearted stories shared, and it isn't unusual to hear laughter ringing from the crowd. During the summer months the benches are carried to shady places outside for the few hours of socializing.

When the ladies are done with cleanup, they likewise settle down for visiting. Popcorn is served to everyone. This popcorn is also brought in by three or four designated families. Often the popcorn is prepackaged in ziplock bags and handed out to individuals. It seems the children know about when popcorn gets served, and they start coming by at the right time to take a bag. Some hosts go a little further in serving the people by stocking a cooler with ice and soft drinks and serving them with the popcorn.

Sometimes the hosts of the church service invite family members or friends from other districts to stay for the afternoon and evening meal. It isn't unusual to have ten to twenty other families visiting from some other church district. In this community of two hundred church districts, services are held every other Sunday, which allows people to visit other church districts on the in-between Sunday.

By 2:00 or 2:30 p.m. everyone is leaving the scene of the church service. Some go directly home, and others stop at other places to visit the housebound, elderly, or newborn babies.

RECIPES FOR MAIN DISHES

TIPS FOR COOKING

* For golden-brown fried chicken, roll pieces in powdered milk instead of flour.
* Toast cheese sandwiches in a frying pan lightly greased with bacon fat for a delightful new flavor.

Katelyn Albrecht, Monticello, KY

* When baking a pie, the crust will get brown before the pie is done. Take a foil pie pan and cut a 6-inch circle out of the middle. Then put the pan upside down over your baking pie. The pie will finish baking, but the crust will not get overdone.
* When you see fat rise to the top of your casserole or noodles, take a paper towel and lay it over the food to soak up the grease. Peel off paper towel and throw away.

Mary K. Bontrager, Middlebury, IN

* If you are thickening fruit, add a pinch of salt. It takes less sugar and brings out the flavor better.

Susie Kinsinger, Fredericktown, OH

BREAKFAST CASSEROLE (GLUTEN-FREE)

Tater tots
1 pound bulk sausage, fried
Ham, cubed
8 eggs, scrambled

Shredded cheddar cheese
White sauce
Bacon (optional)
Corn chips, crushed fine

Grease a 9x13-inch pan. Layer ingredients in order given. Bake at 350 degrees for 30 minutes or until heated through.

WHITE SAUCE:

2 cups milk
2 heaping tablespoons
   cornstarch
4 tablespoons butter

½ teaspoon sea salt
¼ teaspoon pepper
1 cup sour cream

In saucepan, stir milk into cornstarch until smooth. Add butter, salt, and pepper. Cook until thickened, stirring constantly. Let boil 1 minute on low heat. Remove from heat. Mix in sour cream.

Julia Troyer, Fredericksburg, OH

MUSHROOM SAUSAGE STRATA

1 pound pork sausage
10 slices bread, cubed
1 (4 ounce) can mushroom
  stems and pieces, drained
½ cup shredded cheddar
  cheese

½ cup shredded Swiss cheese
6 eggs, lightly beaten
1 cup milk
1 teaspoon Worcestershire
  sauce
½ teaspoon pepper

In skillet, cook sausage over medium heat until no longer pink; drain. Place bread cubes in greased 9x13-inch baking dish. Sprinkle sausage over bread, followed by mushrooms and cheeses. In bowl, combine remaining ingredients; pour over top. Cover and refrigerate overnight. Remove from refrigerator 30 minutes before baking. Bake uncovered at 350 degrees for 35 to 40 minutes, or until knife inserted near center comes out clean. Yield: 8 to 10 servings.

A good breakfast casserole when serving a crowd. Can add more eggs and milk to make more servings.

Mattie Petersheim, Junction City, OH

Breakfast Haystack

Biscuits, crumbled
Sausage gravy
Fried potatoes
Bacon, fried and crumbled

Sausage, fried and crumbled
Scrambled eggs
Cheese sauce

Layer ingredients onto individual plates in order given for a delicious haystack breakfast.

Mary Ellen Wengerd, Campbellsville, KY

Grits and Ham Casserole

9 cups milk
2¼ cups quick-cooking grits
4½ cups chopped ham
3 cups shredded cheddar
    cheese
9 eggs, lightly beaten

6 green onions, chopped
1 tablespoon parsley flakes
1½ teaspoons garlic powder
1½ teaspoons salt
¾ teaspoon pepper

In large pot, bring milk to a boil. Stir in grits. Simmer until thick, stirring often for about 5 minutes. Stir in remaining ingredients. Pour into greased 4-quart baking dish. Bake at 375 degrees for 25 minutes until set.

Anna M. Byler, Clymer, PA

SAUSAGE GRAVY

1 pound bulk sausage
½ cup flour
2 tablespoons milk

Dash Worcestershire sauce
Salt and pepper to taste

Fry sausage. Sprinkle with flour and mix together. Add milk and Worcestershire sauce. Stir until mixture thickens. Thin with more milk to desired thickness. Season with salt and pepper. Serve over biscuits.

Verna Stutzman, Navarre, OH

BEST BEEF ROAST

1 can cream of mushroom
  soup
½ cup water
¼ cup brown sugar
1 teaspoon dry mustard
1 teaspoon salt

1 medium onion, chopped
1 tablespoon Worcestershire
  sauce
2 tablespoons vinegar
4- to 5-pound beef roast

Mix first 8 ingredients together. Pour over roast. Bake covered at 350 degrees for 2 hours, then at 250 degrees for another 4 hours.

Anna M. Byler, Clymer, PA

DUTCH OVEN STEW

2 large packages California
  blend vegetables
3 pounds chicken breasts,
  cubed
1 onion, sliced

1 (16 ounce) bottle Italian
  dressing
1 (16 ounce) bottle vinaigrette
  dressing

Place ingredients in Dutch oven. Add water to cover halfway up stew. Bake at 350 degrees with lid on for 50 to 60 minutes until tender. Also can be cooked outside over a campfire.

Susie Hostetler, New Concord, OH

CHICKEN BUNDLES

1 (8 ounce) package cream
   cheese, softened
½ teaspoon garlic salt
¼ cup dried minced onion

8 boneless chicken breasts
   (about 8 ounces each)
16 strips bacon

Mix cream cheese, garlic salt, and minced onion. Fold chicken breast in half and place 1 tablespoon cream cheese mixture in fold of chicken. Wrap 2 strips bacon around each breast, first one direction then the other. Secure ends with toothpick on top. Bake at 350 degrees for 1 hour. Yield: 4 to 8 servings.

This is an elegant looking entrée that doesn't take a lot of time to prepare.

Kari Danette Petersheim, Fredericktown, OH

Chicken Rice Casserole

4 cups cooked rice
¼ cup melted butter
¼ cup flour
1 teaspoon seasoned salt
¼ teaspoon pepper
2 teaspoons chicken bouillon
½ teaspoon garlic powder
2 cups milk
1 package California blend vegetables, cooked and drained

5 cups diced grilled chicken breast
12 ounces Velveeta cheese
1 cup milk
2 cups sour cream
¼ cup melted butter
1 sleeve Ritz crackers, crushed

Put rice in bottom of 9x13-inch pan. In saucepan, mix ¼ cup melted butter, flour, seasoned salt, pepper, bouillon, garlic powder, and 2 cups milk, and heat until thickened. Pour over rice. Layer on vegetables and chicken. In saucepan, melt cheese in 1 cup milk. Remove from heat; add sour cream. Pour over chicken. Mix butter and cracker crumbs. Bake at 350 degrees for 25 to 30 minutes, until heated through.

Jolene Bontrager, Topeka, IN

Chicken Bacon Ranch Casserole

1 box Velveeta cheese
Milk
2 pounds hash browns
1 bottle ranch dressing
1 pound bacon, fried and
  crumbled
4 cups cubed grilled chicken
  breast
½ cup butter
2 cups crushed cornflakes

In saucepan, melt cheese with enough milk to make a medium-thick sauce. Layer half of hash browns in 9x13-inch baking dish, followed by half of ranch dressing, half of bacon, and half of chicken. Pour half of cheese sauce on top. Repeat layers. Melt butter and combine with cornflakes. Top casserole with cornflake mixture. Bake at 350 degrees for 1 hour, or until heated through.

Jolene Bontrager, Topeka, IN

Country Chicken and Biscuits

3 carrots, sliced
½ cup chopped onion
3½ cups cubed potatoes
2½ cups diced chicken
1 bag frozen peas
1½ cups grated Velveeta
  cheese
1 to 2 cans cream of chicken
  soup
Milk
Biscuit dough

Cook carrots, onion, and potatoes in water until tender; drain. Add chicken, peas, cheese, and soup. Add just enough milk to thin to desired sauce thickness. Bake in covered casserole dish at 375 degrees for 20 minutes until hot and bubbly. Top with biscuit dough and bake uncovered for 20 minutes until golden brown.

Ann Schwartz, Salem, IN

Cheddar Chicken Spaghetti

7 ounces uncooked spaghetti, broken
2 cups cubed cooked chicken
2 cups shredded cheddar cheese, divided

1 can cream of chicken soup
1 cup milk
¼ cup diced bell pepper
¼ teaspoon salt
¼ teaspoon pepper

Cook spaghetti according to package directions. Meanwhile in a bowl, combine chicken, 1 cup cheese, soup, milk, bell pepper, salt, and pepper. Drain spaghetti and combine with chicken mixture. Stir to coat. Transfer to 9x13-inch baking dish. Sprinkle with remaining cheese. Bake uncovered at 350 degrees for 20 to 25 minutes or until heated through. Yield: 6 to 8 servings.

B. Saloma D. Yoder, Mercer, MO

Chicken à la King

1½ to 2 cups cubed cooked potatoes
8 ounces noodles, cooked according to package directions
2 cups chopped cooked chicken

Bread crumbs
8 cups chicken gravy
Seasoning of your choice— such as salt, parsley, pepper

Layer potatoes in large casserole dish. Add layer of noodles. Add layer of chicken and then bread crumbs. Pour gravy over all, making it thin enough so your casserole will not be too dry throughout, and season to taste. Bake at 350 degrees for 30 minutes until top is browned.

Esther M. Peachey, Flemingsburg, KY

CHICKEN GUMBO CASSEROLE

9 slices bread, cubed
4 cups chopped cooked
  chicken
¼ cup melted butter
1 cup chicken broth
9 slices Velveeta cheese

1 can cream of mushroom
  soup
½ cup Miracle Whip salad
  dressing
4 eggs, beaten
1 cup milk
1 teaspoon seasoned salt

Combine ingredients in casserole dish. Bake at 350 degrees for 1½ hours. Stir several times while baking.

Mrs. Aaron (Emma) Gingerich, Bremen, OH

Italian Chicken

½ cup Miracle Whip salad
  dressing
½ cup Italian dressing
2 teaspoons garlic powder
⅛ teaspoon red pepper flakes
¼ teaspoon salt
4 chicken breasts, sliced

Mix dressings and seasonings. Coat chicken with mixture and refrigerate 30 minutes. Grill or bake at 350 degrees for 20 minutes or until done.

Mrs. John H. Mullet, Cass City, MI

Chicken Stir-Fry

2 cups chopped broccoli
2 cups chopped cauliflower
2 cups sliced carrots
2 cups chopped green beans
2 cups chunked cooked
  chicken
Salt and pepper to taste
1 can cream of mushroom
  soup
Shredded cheese

In large skillet, cook vegetables and chicken until vegetables are tender and chicken is no longer pink. Season with salt and pepper. Stir in soup and cheese.

This is very easy and very good to take to something like a school picnic. To keep warm, I wrap the skillet or serving dish in a large bath towel.

Mrs. Samuel J. Schwartz, Bryant, IN

Chicken Vegetable Casserole

2 pounds grilled chicken
  breasts, cubed
1 can cream of mushroom
  soup
16 ounces sour cream
1 package California blend
  vegetables, cooked and
  drained
Velveeta cheese, sliced
1 bag tater tots

Place chicken in 9x13-inch pan. Combine soup and sour cream. Pour over chicken. Layer on vegetables, cheese slices, and tater tots. Bake at 350 degrees for 45 minutes.

Jolene Bontrager, Topeka, IN

FROGMORE STEW

THE YUCKY STUFF (BROTH):

1 cup ketchup
1 cup vegetable oil
1 cup vinegar
1 (3 ounce) package crab boil seasoning

¾ cup salt
2 tablespoons pepper
16 cups water

In 20-quart stainless steel pot, combine all ingredients for broth and bring to a boil.

THE GOOD STUFF:

6 to 8 potatoes, cut up
2 pounds baby carrots
12 ears corn on the cob, cut in thirds
4 to 5 pounds sausage links, cut up
5 to 6 pounds chicken tenders, cut up

2 (12 ounce) packages sliced mushrooms
3 large onions, cut in wedges
2 pounds shrimp
1 to 2 green peppers, sliced

Add potatoes, carrots, and corn to boiling broth. Cook 5 minutes. Add sausage; boil 10 minutes. Add chicken; boil 20 minutes. Add mushrooms and onions; boil 10 minutes. Add shrimp and green peppers; boil 5 minutes. Turn off heat. Let sit 5 minutes. Drain off broth when ready to serve.

SAUCES FOR DIPPING:

Ranch dressing

Cocktail sauce

Melted butter

Sour cream

Ketchup

Blossom sauce (page 72)

This meal is great for a cookout with ten to fourteen family members or friends. We put a clean vinyl or plastic tablecloth on the table and just spread everything down the middle of the table alongside bowls of dips. Sit down and dig in.

Kathy Ebersol, Bristolville, OH

Layered Dinner

1½ pounds ground beef
Salt and pepper to taste
¼ cup ketchup
1 head cabbage

6 to 8 cups diced potatoes
4 slices cheese
1½ cups milk

Brown ground beef. Season with salt and pepper. Mix in ketchup. Set aside. Shred ½ head of cabbage into large baking dish. Add half of potatoes. Sprinkle with salt and pepper. Add all of the beef. Cover with cheese slices. Shred remaining cabbage over cheese. Add remaining potatoes. Pour milk over all. Bake at 375 degrees for 1½ to 2 hours.

Anna M. Byler, Clymer, PA

Tater Tot Casserole

3 pounds chicken breasts
Salt and pepper to taste
1 can cream of chicken soup
½ cup milk

32 ounces frozen peas
32 ounces tater tots
Velveeta cheese, sliced

Cut up chicken in small cubes. Cook until tender and season with salt and pepper. Mix soup and water. Add to chicken and pour in bottom of casserole dish. Add peas and tater tots in layers. Bake at 350 degrees for 1½ hours. When heated through, top with cheese slices and return to oven until cheese is completely melted.

Esther Schwartz, Harrisville, PA

BBQ Ribs

Pork or venison rib racks

Place ribs in roaster pan. Fill with water until half of ribs are covered. Cover pan and bake at 300 degrees for 3 hours, or until you can pull out a bone. Cool a little. Place on hot grill. Slather with homemade barbecue sauce.

Barbecue Sauce:

4 (28 ounce) bottles ketchup
4 cups barbecue sauce
1 cup creamy Italian dressing
1 cup creamy French dressing
1 cup brown sugar
1 cup Worcestershire sauce
1 cup corn syrup
2 teaspoons liquid smoke
2 teaspoons onion powder
4 teaspoons paprika
4 teaspoons chili powder
4 teaspoons pepper
6 teaspoons hot sauce
8 teaspoons lemon juice
1 cup vinegar
4 cups water, divided
1½ to 2 cups clear-jel

In large pot, heat all but 2 cups water and clear-jel. Blend water and clear-jel. Add to heated mixture. Bring to a boil, stirring until thickened. Put in jars to keep in refrigerator or to seal in water bath.

This sauce is a great dip for all kinds of meat.

Ribs are great to make ahead and put in an insulated casserole tote to take on a picnic. Make sure to have plenty of wipes on hand. Ribs are finger-licking good.

Kathy Ebersol, Bristolville, OH

EASY PIZZA CASSEROLE

2 cans cream of mushroom
  soup
6 cups cooked homemade
  noodles, divided
2 quarts pizza sauce
4 cups fried sausage
  crumbles

2 cans mushrooms, drained
2 cups shredded cheese (I like
  Colby)
1 cup chopped onion
1 cup chopped green pepper
Pepperoni
Olives

In roaster pan, spread contents of 1 can soup on bottom. Layer on 3 cups noodles. Pour 1 quart pizza sauce over noodles. Add layer of 2 cups sausage crumbles and 1 can mushrooms, then 1 cup cheese, ½ cup onion, and ½ cup green pepper. Layer on some pepperoni and some olives. Repeat layers with remaining ingredients. Bake at 375 degrees for 1 hour.

I usually take this casserole to family gatherings, and it is a big hit. After the casserole is done, I cover the top with foil then put the lid on top of that to keep anything from spilling over the edge. Then I wrap it in a blanket, and it keeps warm until we eat.

Mrs. Martin A. Schmidt, Carlisle, KY

PIZZA BAKE

1 pound ground beef
½ cup chopped onion
1 pint pizza sauce
1 cup Bisquick baking mix,
  divided

1½ cups cheese
2 eggs
1 cup milk

Brown ground beef and onion. Add pizza sauce and 2 tablespoons of Bisquick. Pour into 9x13-inch pan and top with cheese. Mix eggs, milk, and remaining Bisquick. Pour on top. Bake at 350 degrees for 30 minutes.

Anna M. Byler, Clymer, PA

Pizza Pockets

Ground beef, sausage, ham,
  smokies, and/or pepperoni
1½ cups warm water
2 tablespoons yeast
6 tablespoons brown sugar
4½ cups bread flour

Pizza sauce
Shredded cheese
1 teaspoon baking soda
1 cup warm water
Oregano
Butter, melted

Brown any raw meat you plan to use for filling. In a mixing bowl, mix 1½ cups warm water, yeast, brown sugar, and flour. Let rise. Roll out strips of dough. Put pizza sauce down center of each strip of dough. Top with meat of choice and cheese. Fold both sides of dough strip over center. Pinch to close. Cut off extra dough on ends. Dissolve baking soda in 1 cup warm water. Dip pockets in soda water. Place on greased cookie sheet and sprinkle with oregano. Bake at 400 degrees for 20 to 25 minutes until light brown. Brush with melted butter. These are good for school lunch buckets.

Verna Stutzman, Navarre, OH

Chipotle in a Casserole

Chicken:

2 tablespoons lemon juice
1½ teaspoons seasoned salt
1½ teaspoons oregano
1½ teaspoons cumin
1 teaspoon garlic salt

½ teaspoon chili powder
½ teaspoon paprika
2¼ pounds boneless, skinless chicken breasts, cut into strips (about 4½ cups)
2 tablespoons oil

Combine lemon juice and seasonings. Add chicken and toss to coat. Marinate 4 hours or overnight. Fry in oil until no longer pink. (Or you can grill.) Set aside.

Cilantro-Lime Rice:

2 cups rice
1 cup chopped onion
2 tablespoons oil
4 cups water
½ teaspoon pepper
1 teaspoon salt

2 tablespoons lime juice
⅓ cup chopped cilantro
1 teaspoon cumin
1 teaspoon oregano
1 teaspoon garlic powder

Fry rice and onion in oil until onions are soft and rice is brown. Add remaining ingredients. Bring to a boil and simmer 20 minutes. Set aside. If you prefer, replace lime juice and cilantro with 4 teaspoons chicken base.

Beans:

2 (15 ounce) cans black beans
½ teaspoon cumin
1½ teaspoons chili powder

¾ teaspoon lemon pepper
½ teaspoon salt
½ tablespoon chopped cilantro

Drain beans slightly. Add remaining ingredients and mix.

TOPPINGS:

- 2 cups sour cream
- 2 cups shredded cheddar cheese
- 1 pound shredded lettuce
- 3 medium tomatoes, chopped, or 2 cups salsa
- 1 bottle ranch dressing

Put rice in greased 9x13-inch pan. Top with beans. Sprinkle chicken on top. Spread sour cream over chicken. Top with cheese. Bake covered at 350 degrees for 15 minutes. Uncover and bake 15 minutes longer. Serve with lettuce, tomatoes, and ranch dressing. Yield: 12 to 15 servings.

To prep ahead, assemble all without sour cream and cheese. Refrigerate or freeze. Top with sour cream and cheese before baking. If cold, add 15 minutes to baking time.

Phebe Peight, McVeytown, PA

Taco Filled Pasta Shells

2 pounds ground beef
1 (8 ounce) package cream
  cheese, softened
2 envelopes taco seasoning
24 cooked jumbo pasta shells

1 cup salsa
1 cup pizza sauce
1 cup cheddar cheese
1 cup shredded mozzarella
  cheese

Fry beef; drain. Add cream cheese and taco seasoning. Stir until cream is melted.
Fill each shell with meat mixture. Place 12 shells in 9-inch pan. Pour salsa over
top. Place remaining shells on top. Pour pizza sauce over all. Cover with foil
and bake at 350 degrees for 30 minutes. Uncover. Sprinkle with cheese. Bake 15
minutes longer.

These shells can be prepared and frozen for later use. Thaw in refrigerator for 24
hours before baking. Remove shells from container and assemble with salsa, pizza
sauce, and cheese as described above, then bake.

Mrs. Ray Hershberger, Scottville, MI

Deep-Dish Taco Squares

1 pound ground beef
2 cups flour
1 tablespoon baking powder
1 teaspoon salt
⅓ cup margarine
⅔ cup milk
1 cup finely chopped green
pepper
2 tablespoons finely chopped onion
1 cup sour cream
⅔ cup mayonnaise or salad dressing
1 cup shredded cheese

Brown ground beef, drain, and set aside. Mix flour, baking powder, salt, margarine, and milk. Press into bottom of 9x13-inch pan. Bake at 375 degrees for 15 minutes Cover crust with beef. Layer on green pepper and onion. Mix together sour cream, salad dressing, and cheese. Pour on top of pan contents. Bake 25 minutes until light brown.

Rebecca Mast, Gambier, OH

Mexican Chip Casserole

4 pounds ground beef
1 onion, chopped
3 cups instant rice or 4 cups cooked rice
1 quart cooked soup beans
1 quart pizza sauce
1 pint taco sauce
1 to 2 quarts tomato juice
2 pounds shredded cheese
1 pint sour cream
1½ large packages corn chips, crushed

In large skillet, brown beef and onion. Add rice, beans, pizza sauce, taco sauce, tomato juice, cheese, and sour cream. Put in large roaster and bake at 350 degrees for 1 hour. Top with chips. Bake 10 more minutes. More cheese may be added before topping with chips.

Mrs. Esther Miller, Keytesville, MO

Taco Rice

2 pounds ground beef
1 medium onion, chopped
2 envelopes taco seasoning
2 cups rice
1 quart pizza sauce
1 quart tomato juice

2 cups sour cream
2 cups mayonnaise or creamy salad dressing
2 cups shredded mozzarella cheese
4 cups Bisquick baking mix
1¾ cups milk

Fry ground beef and onion until brown. Add taco seasoning. In saucepan, cook rice in pizza sauce and tomato juice until soft. Mix rice with beef and pour into greased large roaster. Mix sour cream, salad dressing, and cheese. Put on top of beef mixture. Combine biscuit mix and milk together. Drop by spoonful or cookie baller on top. Bake covered at 400 degrees for 30 minutes.

Mrs. Eli (Mary) Miller, Andover, OH

Underground Ham Casserole

6 to 8 ham steaks, cooked and chunked
½ cup margarine
¾ cup chopped onion
2 tablespoons Worcestershire sauce
12 ounces noodles or spaghetti, cooked
2 cups milk

3 to 4 cups cubed Velveeta cheese
3 cans cream of mushroom soup
2 pints sour cream
5 quarts mashed potatoes
3 eggs
Bacon, fried and crumbled (optional)

Combine ham, margarine, onion, and Worcestershire sauce. Cook until onions are tender. Place in bottom of roaster pan. Put noodles on top. In saucepan, heat together milk, cheese, and soup until cheese melts. Pour over noodles. Bake at 350 degrees for 1 hour.

Mix sour cream into mashed potatoes. Add eggs. Spread potato mixture over contents of roaster. Sprinkle with bacon. Bake for 20 minutes until set and lightly browned.

Laura R. Schwartz, Bryant, IN

Mock Ham Loaf

1 pound ground beef
½ pound hot dogs, ground
1 cup cracker crumbs

1 egg, beaten
1 teaspoon salt

Mix together, then prepare glaze. Add half of glaze to meat and mix very well. Put into pan and shape into loaf. Pour remaining glaze over meat. Bake at 350 degrees for 1 hour.

Glaze:

¾ cup brown sugar
½ cup water

1 tablespoon vinegar
1 teaspoon mustard

Mix all together.

We use this meat loaf when we serve our meals for groups. People really rave about it. Then they are surprised what the ingredients are. I like to mix this and put it in pans and freeze it. Be sure to thaw completely before putting in the oven. I don't pour on the remaining glaze until I put it in the oven. Enjoy!

Lorene Herschberger, Sullivan, IL

Pigs in the Garden

1½ pounds raw smoked sausage links, cut in 1-inch chunks
5 large potatoes, thinly sliced
2 to 3 carrots, cut in 3-inch sticks

2 cups fresh green beans
1½ cans cream of mushroom soup
¾ cup milk
Salt and pepper to taste
Velveeta cheese, sliced

Arrange sausage to cover bottom of 2-quart casserole dish. Layer vegetables over sausage. Mix together soup, milk, and salt and pepper. Pour over vegetables. Cover with cheese slices. Cover and bake at 350 degrees for 1½ to 2 hours.

Anita Lorraine Petersheim, Fredericktown, OH

SAUSAGE SPAGHETTI PIE

1 pound spaghetti
4 eggs, beaten
⅔ cup Parmesan cheese
1 cup chopped onion
¼ cup butter
2 cups sour cream
2 teaspoons Italian seasoning

2 pounds bulk pork sausage, fried and drained
1 large can marinara sauce or pizza sauce
1 cup shredded mozzarella cheese
½ cup shredded cheddar cheese

Cook spaghetti according to package directions. Drain and place in large bowl. Add eggs and Parmesan cheese. Place in 3 greased pie pans. (Can also be made in one 9x13-inch pan.) Press mixture onto bottom and up sides to form a crust. Set aside. Sauté onion in butter until tender. Remove from heat. Stir in sour cream and Italian seasoning. Spoon into crusts. Mix sausage with marinara sauce. Spoon over sour cream mixture. Sprinkle with shredded cheese. Bake at 350 degrees for 35 to 40 minutes.

Jolene Bontrager, Topeka, IN

AMISH YUM-A-SETTA

2 pounds extra lean ground beef, browned and drained
½ cup diced onion
¼ cup brown sugar
1 can tomato soup

1 can cream of celery soup
16 ounces no-egg noodles, cooked
8 ounces fat-free cheddar cheese

Combine beef, onion, and brown sugar. In deep dish, layer meat mixture, soups, noodles, and cheese. Bake at 350 degrees for 30 minutes.

Mrs. Levi J. Stutzman, West Salem, OH

Fellowship Hot Dish

- 2 pounds ground beef
- 1 tablespoon Italian seasoning
- 1 pound spaghetti or fettuccini noodles
- 2 eggs
- ¼ cup milk
- 1 (32 ounce) jar spaghetti sauce
- 1 onion, finely chopped
- 2 stalks celery, finely chopped
- ½ green pepper, finely chopped
- Oil or butter
- 2 cups shredded mozzarella cheese
- 20 or more slices pepperoni

Brown ground beef with Italian seasoning while at the same time boiling spaghetti. Beat eggs and milk. Toss with drained spaghetti. Spread into greased 9x13-inch baking dish. Top with sauce. Sauté onion, celery, and green pepper in small amount of oil. Mix vegetables into beef. Spread over sauce. Sprinkle with cheese. Dot top with pepperoni slices. May also garnish top with cherry tomatoes, pepper slices, or both. Bake at 350 degrees for 30 minutes. Cut into 10 to 12 squares to serve.

Esther M. Peachey, Flemingsburg, KY

CHEESEBURGER BUNS

Bread dough (make your
  favorite recipe)
2 pounds ground beef
1 tablespoon chopped onion
Salt and pepper to taste
½ cup ketchup

1 tablespoon vinegar
1 tablespoon brown sugar
1 tablespoon
  Worcestershire sauce
American cheese slices
Butter, melted

Set bread dough to rise. Fry ground beef with onion and salt and pepper. Add ketchup, vinegar, brown sugar, and Worcestershire sauce. Simmer 10 to 15 minutes. Punch dough down and divide into 16 pieces. Gently roll out and stretch each piece into 5-inch circle. Fold a half slice of cheese and place in center of dough. Put 3 small tablespoons of beef mixture on top of cheese. Bring outside ends together and seal with a little water. Place seal side down on cookie sheet. Cover and let rise 20 minutes. Bake at 350 degrees until dough is baked. Brush tops with melted butter. Yield: 16 servings.

Mary Ellen Wengerd, Campbellsville, KY

Sloppy Bar-B-Q

2 pounds ground beef
¼ cup minced onion or ¼ teaspoon onion powder
2 teaspoons salt
¼ teaspoon pepper

2 tablespoons brown sugar
½ cup ketchup
1 tablespoon mustard
2 tablespoons flour
½ cup water

Fry ground beef with onion, salt, and pepper. Add brown sugar, ketchup, and mustard. Mix flour and water; add to beef mixture to thicken. Serve on hamburger buns.

Mary K. Bontrager, Middlebury, IN

Barbecue Ham Sandwiches

1 cup ketchup
3 tablespoons lemon juice
¼ cup chopped onion
¼ cup brown sugar

2 tablespoons Worcestershire sauce
1 teaspoon mustard
Celery, chopped (optional)
2 pounds chipped ham slices

In pot, combine all but ham. When hot, add ham and heat through. Serve on buns. Good for crowds. (5 pounds ham will fill 60 buns.)

Alma Gingerich, Irvona, PA

Homemade Sub Sandwiches

1 bottle ranch dressing
12 sandwich rolls (page 37)
2 different sliced meats
Shredded cheese

Bacon, fried and crumbled
Chopped onion
Chopped bell peppers

Spread dressing on sandwich rolls and fill with other ingredients. Wrap each sandwich in foil or parchment paper. Warm in oven at 350 degrees for 15 to 20 minutes.

Katie Miller, Arthur, IL

CHEESY FLORET SOUP

3 cups fresh broccoli florets
3 cups fresh cauliflower
    florets
3 celery ribs, diced
1 small onion, chopped
2 cups water
½ teaspoon celery salt

1 pound ground beef
3 tablespoons butter
3 tablespoons flour
2½ cups milk
1 pound Velveeta cheese
Salt and pepper to taste

In large saucepan, combine broccoli, cauliflower, celery, onion, water, and celery salt. Bring to a boil; reduce heat, cover, and simmer 15 minutes or until vegetables are tender. Meanwhile, brown and drain ground beef. In small saucepan, melt butter. Stir in flour until smooth. Gradually add milk. Bring to a boil. Cook until thickened. Reduce heat. Add cheese and stir until cheese is melted. Combine vegetables, beef, and cheese sauce. Season with salt and pepper.

Vera Jean Hochstetler, Nappanee, IN

World's Best BBQ Burgers

Sauce:

1 cup ketchup
½ cup brown sugar
⅓ cup sugar
¼ cup molasses or maple
    syrup
2 teaspoons mustard

¼ teaspoon salt
1½ teaspoons Worcestershire
    sauce
¼ teaspoon liquid smoke
⅓ cup honey

Mix all together. Store in refrigerator.

Burgers:

¼ cup sauce
1 egg
⅓ cup quick oats
¼ teaspoon onion salt

¼ teaspoon pepper
¼ teaspoon garlic salt
1½ pounds ground beef

In bowl, combine sauce, egg, oats, and spices. Add ground beef and mix well. Shape into 6 patties. Grill, basting with more sauce.

Katie Miller, Arthur, IL

Bierock Casserole

2 pounds ground beef
1 onion, chopped
1 head cabbage, shredded
1 can cream of
    mushroom soup

Salt and pepper to taste
2 cans crescent roll dough
Velveeta cheese, sliced

Brown beef and onion. Drain. Add cabbage and cook until softened. Add soup and salt and pepper. In greased 9x13-inch pan, cover bottom with 1 can dough. Layer with beef mixture. Cover with cheese slices. Top with remaining dough. Bake at 350 degrees for 1 hour.

Mrs. Orie Detweiler, Inola, OK

Rice Pizza

2 cups cooked brown rice	Mushrooms
2 tablespoons butter	Black olives
1 egg, beaten	Shredded cheese
Baked beans	Pizza or Italian seasoning

Mix rice, butter, and egg. Press into bottom of 9x13-inch pan. Top with beans, mushrooms, olives, cheese, and seasoning. Bake at 350 degrees for 30 minutes.

Laura Miller, Mount Vernon, OH

Chowder

2½ cups chopped carrots	1 tablespoon salt
2½ cups chopped celery	¾ teaspoon basil
2 tablespoons oil or chicken fat	⅓ teaspoon oregano
1 tablespoon onion flakes	4 cups cubed potatoes
1 teaspoon garlic salt or ¼ teaspoon garlic powder	2 cups chicken broth

In gallon pot, sauté carrots and celery in oil for about 5 minutes. Add seasonings; mix well. Add potatoes. Sauté another 5 minutes. Add broth and cook until potatoes are just getting tender. Turn off heat. Prepare sauce.

Sauce:

1 tablespoon butter	1 teaspoon salt
1 tablespoon flour	¼ teaspoon pepper
2 cups milk	2 cups diced chicken
4 tablespoons flour	1½- to 2-inch slice Velveeta cheese, cut up

In saucepan, melt butter; add 1 tablespoon flour, stirring well. In shaker jar, mix milk and 4 tablespoons flour. Add to saucepan and heat to boiling. Reduce heat to low and add salt, pepper, and chicken. Add cheese, stirring until melted and hot. Pour over vegetable mixture in first pot.

Esther L. Miller, Fredericktown, OH

Big Batch Texican Chili

1 pound bacon, cut up
3 pounds ground beef
2 medium onions, chopped
1 (6 pound) can stewed
  tomatoes
1 (106 ounce) can tomato
  sauce
1 (48 ounce) can tomato juice
2 (15 ounce) cans kidney
  beans, drained and rinsed
4 cups water

4 cups diced carrots
2 cups diced celery
1 cup diced bell pepper
3 tablespoons parsley flakes
2 tablespoons chili powder
2 tablespoons salt
½ teaspoon pepper
1 teaspoon cumin
1 package chili seasoning
½ cup brown sugar

In skillet, fry bacon, ground beef, and onions; drain. Transfer meat mixture to large, heavy stockpot. Add remaining ingredients. Bring to a boil. Cover and reduce heat to medium-low. Simmer 45 minutes. Uncover and simmer 15 minutes.

Alternate cooking method: Transfer meat mixture to large slow cooker or small electric roaster; add remaining ingredients. Cover and cook on low heat for 8 hours, stirring occasionally. Can uncover the last hour to help reduce liquid.

Tip: I use the 4 cups water to rinse the tomato cans and be sure I get every bit of tomato into the chili.

Lydia Miller, Loudonville, OH

Kabby's Loaded Potato Soup

1 pound bacon, cut up
6 medium potatoes, peeled
  and cut small
2 celery stalks, chopped
1 large onion, chopped

16 ounces sour cream
½ block Velveeta cheese
1 envelope ranch seasoning
Shredded cheese (optional)

Fry bacon. Place potatoes, celery, and onion in pot with enough water to just cover potatoes. Cook until tender. Add sour cream, cheese, and seasoning. Stir until smooth. Add bacon and some bacon grease for great flavor. Serve with a sprinkle of shredded cheese.

This soup is one I make for shut-ins as it is easy to warm back up.

Kathy Ebersol, Bristolville, OH

AMISH DESSERTS

by Amish friend Lydiann Yoder, Andover, OH

In my mother's day you would not find cream cheese and Cool Whip listed in the ingredients of a recipe book. Mom used to tell us how she worked for the family that owned White Brothers' grocery store in Middlefield, Ohio. These people sent extra groceries home with her, and one day she was given a case of cream cheese. They didn't know what to do with it except to spread it on bread.

Dessert recipes were mostly vanilla cracker pudding and fruit dumplings. Caramel and brown sugar dumplings were my dad's favorite dessert. He would say he needed to go on his knees and beg for some. In later years, he was diabetic and wasn't allowed any sweets. He would get so hungry for his favorite dessert.

When Dad fell at work and shattered his kneecap, my mother, wanting to do something nice for him, made him some. She was glad she did, because a few days later he died from blood clots.

I have included the recipe for brown sugar dumplings in his memory (page 180).

RECIPES FOR DESSERTS

TIPS FOR CLEANING UP

♦ Put a roll of trash bags in the bottom of a wastebasket. It is always there when you take the full bag out and need another one.

Esther L. Miller, Fredericktown, OH

♦ When baking cookies and you run out of space on your cooling racks, use newspaper. Lay out 3 sheets thick. Put cookies on to cool. This works well for me when I have lots of church cookies to bake. When done, just roll up the newspaper for quick and easy cleanup.

♦ When you buy cheese by bulk and want to freeze leftovers after a gathering, put wax paper between each slice of cheese and freeze. When you want to thaw some, take out of freezer and put in refrigerator to thaw completely and it won't be crumbly. The wax paper will let slices come apart easily.

Mary K. Bontrager, Middlebury, IN

♦ When you empty your pots of food, always put some hot water in the pot and replace the lid tightly. Set aside. Your pots will be much easier to clean.

♦ Never scrub a cast iron kettle or skillet with a scouring pad. The protective coating will be removed and food will stick.

Susie Kinsinger, Fredericktown, OH

♦ Bleach your cutting board with lemon juice. It will keep the bad smells away. Baking soda works too. Just rub it in.

Katelyn Albrecht, Monticello, KY

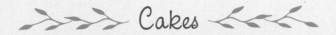

Cakes

CHEESECAKE

1 large box gelatin (your
  flavor choice)
1 cup hot water
1 sleeve graham crackers
4 tablespoons butter

1 (8 ounce) package cream
  cheese, softened
1 cup sugar
1 teaspoon vanilla
1 large can evaporated milk
  or 1½ cups cream, chilled

Dissolve gelatin in hot water; chill in refrigerator until it just starts to thicken. Meanwhile, crush graham crackers and mix in butter. Press into bottom of 9x13-inch pan, saving ⅛ cup for garnish. In bowl, combine cream cheese and sugar, then vanilla. Beat cold milk until thickened. Add to cream cheese mixture, then add combined milk mixture to gelatin. Beat until fluffy. Pour over graham cracker crust. Sprinkle remaining crumbs on top. Refrigerate until set.

I like to take this to church suppers.

Mrs. Ervin (Susan) Byler, Crab Orchard, KY

DARK CHOCOLATE CAKE

1¾ cups flour
2 cups sugar
¾ cup cocoa powder
1½ teaspoons baking powder
1 teaspoon salt

2 eggs
1 cup milk
½ cup vegetable oil
2 teaspoons vanilla
1 cup hot water

Mix all ingredients well. Batter will be very thin. Pour into greased 9x13-inch pan and bake at 350 degrees for 35 to 40 minutes. It is a very moist cake.

Sara Hochstetler, Keytesville, MO

FROZEN CHEESECAKE

CRUST:

6 tablespoons brown sugar
1½ sleeves graham crackers, crushed (2½ cups crumbs)

¾ cup butter, melted and slightly browned

Mix together and press into 9x13-inch pan.

FILLING:

2 (8 ounce) packages cream cheese
1 cup sugar
1 (8 ounce) tub whipped topping

4 eggs, beaten*
1 teaspoon vanilla

Blend together well and spread over crust. Freeze until ready to serve. Before serving, spread 1 quart of your favorite pie filling over top.

I really like this recipe as it can be fixed beforehand and frozen. Can be taken to cookouts, church dinner, and other places.

*Editor's note: use raw eggs with caution.

Daniel and Fannie Miller, New Concord, OH

BANANA NUT CAKE

⅔ cup shortening
2½ cups flour
1⅔ cups sugar
1¼ teaspoons baking powder
1 teaspoon baking soda

1 teaspoon salt
1¼ cups mashed fully ripe bananas
⅔ cup buttermilk
2 eggs
⅔ cup chopped walnuts

In large bowl, stir shortening to soften. Stir in dry ingredients. Add bananas and half of buttermilk. Mix until flour is dampened. Beat vigorously for 2 minutes. Add remaining buttermilk and eggs; beat 2 minutes. Fold in nuts. Pour into greased and floured 9x13-inch pan. Bake at 350 degrees for 35 to 40 minutes. Cool. Ice with your favorite powdered sugar icing.

Betty Miller, Decatur, IN

LEMON CHEESECAKE

CRUST:

1½ cups quick oats
½ cup chopped pecans
⅓ cup brown sugar

1 teaspoon cinnamon
¼ cup butter, melted

Mix all together. Put on cookie sheet and bake at 350 degrees for 12 to 15 minutes. Do not let crumbs get too brown. Cool. Spread crumbs into 9x13-inch pan.

FILLING:

½ cup lemon gelatin
¾ cup boiling water
¾ cup cold water
2 (8 ounce) packages cream cheese

¾ cup powdered sugar
1 (12 ounce) tub whipped topping
Blueberry or black raspberry pie filling

Dissolve gelatin in boiling water, stirring. Add cold water. Set in refrigerator until slightly jelled. Beat cream cheese and powdered sugar until smooth and creamy. Beat in gelatin. Fold in whipped topping. Spread over crust. Freeze. Serve with pie filling.

This is a handy dessert as it can be made ahead and frozen. Then it can be served frozen or allowed to completely thaw before serving. It is also attractive when made and served in individual dishes.

Kathryn Troyer, Rutherford, TN

White Chocolate Raspberry Cheesecake

1½ cups graham cracker crumbs
1 cup sugar, divided
⅓ cup butter, melted
3 (8 ounce) packages cream cheese, softened
⅓ cup sour cream
3 tablespoons flour
1 teaspoon vanilla
3 eggs, lightly beaten
1 (10 ounce) package white or vanilla baking chips
¼ cup raspberry pie filling

In small bowl, combine cracker crumbs, ¼ cup sugar, and butter. Press into bottom of greased 9-inch pan. In large bowl, beat cream cheese with ¾ cup sugar until smooth. Beat in sour cream, flour, and vanilla. Add eggs. Beat on slow speed just until combined. Fold in baking chips. Pour batter over crust. Drop pie filling by teaspoons over batter. Cut through batter with knife to swirl in filling. Bake at 325 degrees for 80 to 85 minutes. Carefully run knife around edges to loosen. Cool for 1 hour. Refrigerate overnight. Yield: 12 servings.

Esther Mast, Gambier, OH

Angel Food Cake (Gluten-Free)

2 cups egg whites
½ teaspoon sea salt
1 teaspoon clear vanilla
2 teaspoons cream of tartar
¾ cup sugar
¾ cup white rice flour
¾ cup tapioca starch
½ cup sugar

In mixer, beat egg whites, salt, vanilla, and cream of tartar until soft peaks form. Add ¾ cup sugar gradually until stiff peaks form. In bowl, mix rice flour, tapioca starch, and ½ cup sugar. Lower mixer speed and slowly add dry mixture to egg white mixture, mixing until blended. Pour into tube or oblong angel food cake pan. Bake at 350 degrees for 50 to 60 minutes. Do not overbake. Invert to cool.

Julia Troyer, Fredericksburg, OH

Fresh Apple Cake

3 cups flour
¾ teaspoon baking soda
1½ teaspoons baking powder
½ teaspoon salt
½ teaspoon cinnamon
½ teaspoon nutmeg
¼ teaspoon mace

1⅓ cups sugar
1⅓ cups oil
3 eggs, beaten
2 teaspoons vanilla
3 cups shredded apples
¾ cup chopped pecans

Combine flour, baking soda, baking powder, salt, cinnamon, nutmeg, and mace. In large bowl, combine sugar, oil, eggs, and vanilla; mix well. Add flour mixture, stirring well. Stir in apples and pecans. Batter will be stiff. Spoon batter into well-greased and floured 10-inch Bundt pan. Bake at 325 degrees for 1 hour and 15 minutes, or until wooden toothpick comes out clean. Cool cake in pan for 10 minutes. Remove from pan and cool completely. Store in airtight container. Can be dribbled with caramel frosting over top and sides.

Esther L. Miller, Fredericktown, OH

Easy Mix Chocolate Cake

3 cups flour
2 cups sugar
½ cup cocoa powder
½ teaspoon baking powder
2 teaspoons baking soda

1 cup hot water
1 cup lard
2 eggs
1 cup milk

Mix dry ingredients, then add remaining ingredients in order given. Pour batter on large greased cookie sheet. Bake at 350 degrees for 30 minutes or until toothpick inserted in center comes out clean. Cool. Cover with icing.

Icing:

2 cups powdered sugar
½ cup cocoa powder

1 tablespoon creamy peanut butter
Water

Beat together with enough water to reach spreading consistency.

Mrs. Samuel J. Schwartz, Bryant, IN

Mexican Chocolate Chiffon Cake

¾ cup hot coffee
⅓ cup cocoa powder
1¾ cups sifted flour
1⅔ cups sugar
½ teaspoon salt

1½ teaspoons baking soda
½ cup vegetable oil
2 teaspoons vanilla
7 eggs, separated
½ teaspoon cream of tartar

Blend hot coffee and cocoa powder; set aside to cool. Sift together flour, sugar, salt, and baking soda. Place in large bowl and make well in center. Add oil, vanilla, 7 egg yolks, and coffee mixture to well. Beat until smooth. In large bowl, beat 7 egg whites with cream of tartar until very stiff. Pour chocolate mixture gradually over egg whites, gently folding in until blended. Pour batter into 10-inch tube cake pan. Bake at 325 degrees for 55 minutes, then increase heat to 350 degrees and bake 10 to 15 minutes. Invert pan to cool completely. Run knife around pan to release cake and invert onto a plate. Drizzle with warm frosting.

Frosting:

1 cup sugar
1 tablespoon cornstarch
2 tablespoons cocoa powder
½ teaspoon salt

1 cup boiling water
1 teaspoon margarine
1 teaspoon vanilla

In saucepan, place the sugar, cornstarch, cocoa powder, and salt. Pour boiling water over, mixing in. Bring mixture to a boil. Remove from heat and add margarine and vanilla, stirring until smooth.

Susan R. Schwartz, Bryant, IN

GRANDMA'S CHOCOLATE ZUCCHINI CAKE

½ cup shortening
2 cups sugar
2 eggs
2⅔ cups flour
1½ scant teaspoons baking
 soda

3 teaspoons baking powder
½ teaspoon salt
½ cup cocoa powder
2 cups chopped zucchini
2 teaspoons vanilla
2 cups hot water

Blend shortening, sugar, and eggs. In separate bowl, combine flour, baking soda, baking powder, salt, and cocoa powder. Add dry mixture to first mixture. Add zucchini and vanilla. Stir in hot water. Pour into greased and floured 9x13-inch pan. Bake between 350 degrees for 25 to 30 minutes.

Mrs. Aaron (Emma) Gingerich, Bremen, OH

CHERRY COFFEE CAKE

1 cup butter
1½ cups sugar
4 eggs
1 teaspoon vanilla

3 cups flour
1½ teaspoons baking powder
½ teaspoon salt
1 can cherry pie filling

Cream together butter and sugar. Add eggs one at a time. Beat well after each. Add vanilla. Sift together flour, baking powder, and salt. Add to creamed mixture. Spread two-thirds of dough on large greased jelly roll pan (10.5x15.5-inch). Cover with pie filling. Spoon remaining dough on top. Bake at 350 degrees for 30 to 40 minutes. Drizzle with glaze while warm.

GLAZE:

1½ cups powdered sugar
2 tablespoons melted butter

½ teaspoon vanilla
Warm milk

Blend powdered sugar, butter, and vanilla. Add just enough milk to make thin glaze for drizzling.

Judith Miller, Fredericktown, OH

SOUR CREAM COFFEE CAKE

½ cup butter
1 cup sugar
2 eggs
1 cup sour cream
1 teaspoon baking soda

1½ teaspoons vanilla
2 cups flour, divided
1 teaspoon baking powder
½ teaspoon salt

In mixing bowl, cream butter and sugar well. Beat in eggs, one at a time. In small bowl, combine sour cream with baking soda and vanilla. Combine flour, baking powder, and salt. To creamed mixture, add 1 cup flour mixture, then sour cream, then remaining flour. Pour batter in 2 greased foil pie pans. Put crumb topping on top and bake at 350 degrees for 25 minutes or until cakes spring back when centers are touched. Slice both cakes through middle and coat with cream filling.

CRUMB TOPPING:

½ cup flour
½ cup brown sugar

1 teaspoon cinnamon
3 tablespoons melted butter

Mix together until crumbly.

CREAM FILLING:

2 beaten egg whites
2 teaspoons vanilla
½ cup shortening

2 tablespoons marshmallow
  crème
2 cups powdered sugar

Combine ingredients and mix well.

Rachel D. Miller, Millersburg, OH

PEACHES-AND-CREAM COFFEE CAKE

⅔ cup flour
1 teaspoon baking powder
½ teaspoon salt
1 egg

½ cup milk
3 tablespoons melted butter
1 large can sliced peaches or
    2½ cups sweetened fresh
    peaches

Mix flour, baking powder, and salt. Add egg, milk, and butter. Beat. Pour into well-greased 8-inch round pan. Drain peaches, reserving juice. Arrange peaches over batter.

FILLING:

1 (8 ounce) package cream
    cheese, softened

½ cup sugar
3 tablespoons peach juice

Cream together and spoon over peaches.

TOPPING:

1 tablespoon sugar

½ teaspoon cinnamon

Blend and sprinkle over filling. Bake at 350 degrees for 35 minutes.

Betty Miller, Decatur, IN

Best-Yet Oatmeal Cake

1¾ cups boiling water
1 cup quick oats
½ cup butter
⅓ cup sugar
1 cup brown sugar
3 eggs

1¾ cups flour
1 teaspoon baking soda
1 teaspoon baking powder
½ teaspoon salt
1 teaspoon vanilla

Put boiling water in bowl; add oats and butter. Cover and let stand 15 minutes. Add sugars and eggs; beat well. Combine flour, baking soda, baking powder, and salt. Add to oat mixture. Add vanilla. Mix well. Bake in greased 9x13-inch pan at 350 degrees for 30 to 40 minutes. When done, immediately put on topping.

Topping:

6 tablespoons butter
1 cup brown sugar
¼ cup milk

¾ cup shredded coconut
¾ cup chopped pecans

In saucepan, mix topping ingredients and cook over low heat until it bubbles. Spread over baked cake. Put under oven broiler at high heat for 2 minutes. Check that it doesn't get too dark.

Esther L. Miller, Fredericktown, OH

Oatmeal Chocolate Chip Cake

1¾ cups boiling water
1 cup quick oats
1 cup sugar
1 cup brown sugar
½ cup butter or margarine, softened
3 eggs

1¾ cups flour
1 teaspoon baking soda
1 teaspoon cocoa powder
¼ teaspoon salt
12 ounces chocolate chips, divided
¾ cup chopped walnuts

In mixing bowl, pour boiling water over oats and let stand 10 minutes. Add sugars and butter, stirring until butter melts. Add eggs, one at a time, mixing well after each addition. Sift flour, baking soda, cocoa powder, and salt together. Add to first mixture, mixing well. Stir in half of chocolate chips. Pour into greased 9x13-inch baking pan. Sprinkle top of batter with walnuts and remaining chips. Bake at 350 degrees for about 40 minutes until done.

Anna M. Yoder, Mercer, MO

Pineapple Sheet Cake

2 cups sugar
2 cups flour
2 teaspoons baking soda

2 eggs
1 (20 ounce) can crushed pineapple

Mix all together and bake at 350 degrees for 35 minutes on greased cookie sheet. Ice while warm.

Icing:

1 (8 ounce) package cream cheese, softened
¼ cup butter

1 teaspoon vanilla
1 cup powdered sugar

Blend well.

Velma Schrock, Goshen, IN

Shoofly Cake

4 cups flour
2 cups brown sugar
1 cup butter, softened

2 cups boiling water
1 cup molasses
1 teaspoon baking soda

Combine flour, brown sugar, and butter; mix well. Reserve 1 cup crumbs for topping. Mix together boiling water, molasses, and baking soda. Gradually add flour mixture until well blended. Pour into greased 9x13-inch pan. Sprinkle with reserved crumbs. Bake at 325 degrees for 45 to 50 minutes.

Phebe Peight, McVeytown, PA

White Cake

2⅓ cups sifted flour
3½ teaspoons baking powder
1 teaspoon salt
¾ cup sugar
⅔ cup vegetable oil
½ cup milk

¾ cup water
2 teaspoons vanilla
4 egg whites
¼ teaspoon cream of tartar
¾ cup sugar

Mix flour, baking powder, salt, and ¾ cup sugar in large bowl. Add oil, milk, water, and vanilla. Stir very well. Beat egg whites and cream of tartar until stiff, then add ¾ cup sugar. Fold into cake batter. Bake in 2 well-greased 9-inch round pans at 350 degrees for 30 or 40 minutes.

For chocolate cake, omit 2 tablespoons flour and replace with 2 tablespoons cocoa powder.

We use this recipe to make wedding cakes. Light and moist and very good.

Jonas and Sarah Gingerich, Junction City, OH

White Caramel Swiss Roll Cake

1¾ cups flour
⅔ cup sugar
1 (3 ounce) box instant vanilla
pudding mix
2 teaspoons baking powder

½ teaspoon salt
2 eggs
1¼ cups milk
½ cup vegetable oil
1 teaspoon vanilla

Combine flour, sugar, pudding mix, baking powder, and salt. Add eggs, milk, oil, and vanilla. Mix well. Pour into well-greased and floured 10x15-inch pan. Bake at 350 degrees for 15 to 20 minutes until done. Cool slightly, then turn out onto clean dish towel dusted with powdered sugar. Roll cake starting from shortest end. Cool completely.

Filling:

1 (8 ounce) package cream
cheese, softened
⅔ cup brown sugar
⅛ teaspoon salt

1 teaspoon vanilla
1 (8 ounce) tub whipped
topping

Mix cream cheese, sugar, salt, and vanilla until light and fluffy. Fold in whipped topping. Unroll cake and spread with filling. Re-roll cake.

Frosting:

½ cup butter, softened
1 cup brown sugar

1 cup sour cream

Bring butter and brown sugar to a boil for 2 minutes. Cool for 30 minutes. Stir in sour cream. Cool completely in refrigerator before spreading over cake roll.

For a shortcut, use a white cake mix for the cake portion.

Jolene Bontrager, Topeka, IN

WHITE JELLY ROLL

¾ cup cake flour
1 cup sugar, divided
1 cup egg whites (8 to 10 eggs)

½ teaspoon salt
1 teaspoon cream of tartar
1 teaspoon vanilla

Sift flour and ⅔ cup sugar 4 times. In separate bowl, combine egg whites, salt, cream of tartar, and vanilla. Beat until stiff. Beat in remaining ⅓ cup sugar 2 tablespoons at a time. Beat until you can hold bowl upside down without contents dumping out. Use a big spoon and slowly blend in sifted ingredients 2 tablespoons at a time. Spread on wax paper–lined cake pan and bake at 350 degrees for 20 to 25 minutes. Cool 10 minutes before taking off wax paper and rolling up. Cool. Unroll and spread with filling, then pie filling if desired. Roll back up.

FILLING:

1 cup water
4 tablespoons flour
4 tablespoons sugar
¼ teaspoon salt

1 egg yolk
1 teaspoon vanilla
1 teaspoon butter
Fruit pie filling (optional)

Bring water to a boil. In the meantime, mix flour, sugar, salt, egg yolk, and vanilla. Add butter to water and melt. Slowly add flour mixture to water. Cook for 5 minutes. Cool.

B. Saloma D. Yoder, Mercer, MO

Yum-Yum Cupcakes

1 (8 ounce) package cream
  cheese
1 egg
2⅓ cups sugar, divided
Dash salt
8 ounces chocolate chips
3 cups flour

½ cup cocoa powder
2 teaspoons vanilla
2 teaspoons baking soda
2 tablespoons vinegar
⅔ cup vegetable oil
2 cups water

Cream together cream cheese, egg, ⅓ cup sugar, and salt. Add chocolate chips. Set aside. Combine remaining 2 cups sugar, flour, cocoa powder, vanilla, baking soda, vinegar, oil, and water. Fill baking cups half full of batter. Add 1 spoonful cream cheese mixture to each cup and bake at 350 degrees for 20 to 25 minutes.

Mrs. Emanuel Schmidt, Carlisle, KY

Fluffy Cream Cheese Frosting

4 ounces cream cheese,
  softened
1 (7 ounce) jar marshmallow
  crème

1 (8 ounce) tub whipped
  topping

Beat cream cheese and marshmallow crème until well blended. Fold in whipped topping. Great for topping cupcakes.

Variations:

Lemon—add 2 tablespoons lemon juice and 1 tablespoon lemon zest

Chocolate—add 3 ounces semisweet chocolate, melted and slightly cooled

Coconut—add ½ cup toasted coconut

Jolene Bontrager, Topeka, IN

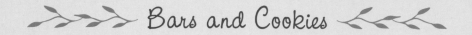

STRAWBERRY TWINKIES

1 box strawberry cake mix
1 (3 ounce) box instant white
  chocolate pudding mix
1 cup water
4 eggs
½ cup oil

Mix all ingredients. Divide into two 9x13-inch pans. Bake at 350 degrees for 15 to 20 minutes. Cool.

FILLING:

1 (8 ounce) package cream
  cheese, softened
1 cup powdered sugar
¾ cup milk
1 (3 ounce) box instant white
  chocolate pudding mix
1 cup whipped topping

Cream together cream cheese and powdered sugar. Add milk and pudding mix. Stir well. Add whipped topping. Spread filling over 1 cake. Place second cake on top. Cut into rectangles.

Vera Jean Hochstetler, Nappanee, IN

FAVORITE BROWNIES

3 cups butter, softened
6 cups sugar (or less)
2 tablespoons vanilla
12 eggs
4¾ cups flour
2 cups cocoa powder
2 teaspoons baking powder
2 teaspoons salt
2 cups chocolate chips

In large bowl, mix ingredients in order given. Pour into 2 large greased jelly roll pans. Sprinkle 1 cup chocolate chips on each pan. Bake at 350 degrees for 40 minutes. Do not overbake.

Great treat for family gatherings or church carry-ins, or to freeze for later.

Elizabeth Shetler, Brinkhaven, OH

Speedy Brownies

2 cups sugar
½ cup cocoa powder
5 eggs
1 teaspoon vanilla

1¾ cups flour
1 teaspoon salt
1 cup vegetable oil
1 cup semisweet chocolate
 chips

In mixing bowl, combine all but chocolate chips; beat until smooth. Pour into greased 9x13-inch pan. Sprinkle with chocolate chips. Bake at 350 degrees for 30 minutes or until toothpick inserted near center comes out clean. Cool on wire rack. Yield: 3 dozen.

These are simple and easy to make and ideal to take along to a finger-food dinner or a picnic.

Martha Petersheim, Junction City, OH

CHURCH SUGAR COOKIES

1 cup sugar
2 cups brown sugar
2 cups vegetable oil
4 eggs, beaten
2 cups buttermilk or sour cream
1 tablespoon vanilla
1 (3 ounce) box instant vanilla pudding mix
2 tablespoons baking powder
½ teaspoon salt
2 teaspoons baking soda
6½ cups flour

Cream together sugars, oil, and eggs. Add buttermilk, then vanilla and pudding mix. Add remaining ingredients. Sprinkle flour lightly onto cookie sheet. Drop cookie dough by spoonfuls onto cookie sheet. Sprinkle cookies generously with sugar. Bake at 350 degrees for 12 to 14 minutes. Cookies are done when centers spring back when touched.

Mary K. Bontrager, Middlebury, IN

Peanut Butter Truffle Brownies

1 box fudge brownie mix
  or your favorite brownie
  recipe
½ cup butter, softened
½ cup creamy peanut butter

2 cups powdered sugar
2 teaspoons milk
¼ cup butter
1 cup semisweet chocolate
  chips

Bake brownies in 9x13-inch pan. Cool completely. In medium bowl, beat ½ cup butter, peanut butter, powdered sugar, and milk. Spread over brownies. In small saucepan, melt ¼ cup butter over low heat. Add chocolate chips, stirring until melted. Cool 10 minutes. Spread over peanut butter mixture.

Jolene Bontrager, Topeka, IN

Texas Brownies

2 cups flour
2 cups sugar
½ cup margarine or butter
½ cup shortening
1 cup strong-brewed coffee

¼ cup dark unsweetened
  cocoa powder
½ cup buttermilk
2 eggs
1 teaspoon baking soda
1 teaspoon vanilla

In large bowl, mix flour and sugar together. In saucepan, combine margarine, shortening, coffee, and cocoa powder. Stir and heat to boiling. Pour boiling mixture over flour. Mix. Add remaining ingredients; mix well. Pour into greased jelly roll pan. Bake at 400 degrees for 20 minutes or until toothpick inserted in center comes out clean. Frost when cool.

Frosting:

⅓ cup butter, softened
1 (8 ounce) package cream
  cheese, softened

½ cup cocoa powder
1 tablespoon vanilla
4 cups powdered sugar

Cream butter and cream cheese together. Add cocoa powder and vanilla; mix well. Gradually add powdered sugar. Beat until smooth.

Anna Mast, Gambier, OH

Soft Chocolate Chip Cookies

1 cup sugar	4 teaspoons baking soda
2 cups brown sugar	4 teaspoons baking powder
1 cup lard	½ teaspoon salt
4 eggs	2 cups sweet or sour milk
6 cups flour	2 cups chocolate chips

Mix sugars and lard. Add eggs; beat well. In separate bowl, combine flour, baking soda, baking powder, and salt. Add dry mixture to creamed mixture alternately with milk. Mix in chocolate chips. Drop by spoonfuls onto lightly greased cookie sheets. Bake at 375 degrees for 8 to 10 minutes—just until no impression remains when lightly touched.

Rebecca Mast, Gambier, OH

Fudge Marshmallow Cookies

½ cup lard or shortening	½ cup cocoa powder
⅔ cup sugar	¼ teaspoon salt
1 egg	½ teaspoon baking soda
1 teaspoon vanilla	⅛ teaspoon baking powder
¼ cup milk	18 large marshmallows, halved
1¾ cups flour	

Cream lard and sugar. Add egg, vanilla, and milk. Add flour, cocoa powder, salt, baking soda, and baking powder. Mix well. Drop by spoonfuls onto greased cookie sheet. Bake at 350 degrees for 8 to 10 minutes. Do not overbake. Remove from oven and top each cookie with a marshmallow half. Return to oven for 45 seconds. Cool and frost. Yield: 3 dozen.

FROSTING:

2 cups powdered sugar	4 to 5 tablespoons light cream
5 tablespoons cocoa powder	½ cup chopped pecans
3 tablespoons melted butter	

Beat together powdered sugar, cocoa powder, butter, and 4 tablespoons cream. Add more cream to reach spreading consistency. Spread frosting on each cookie and sprinkle with nuts.

Esther L. Miller, Fredericktown, OH

Classic Chocolate Chip Cookies

4 cups butter
1 cup sugar
3 cups brown sugar
8 eggs
4 teaspoons vanilla

4 (6.5 ounce) boxes instant
  vanilla pudding mix
9 cups flour
4 teaspoons baking soda
1 teaspoon baking powder
4 cups chocolate chips

Cream together butter, sugars, eggs, and vanilla. Add remaining ingredients. Drop by spoonfuls onto cookie sheets. Bake at 375 degrees for 9 minutes.

These are a good seller at our produce and bake stand.

Jonas and Sarah Gingerich, Junction City, OH

MOLASSES CRÈME COOKIES

2¾ cups shortening
5 cups brown sugar
4 eggs
1 cup light molasses
4 teaspoons cinnamon
⅛ teaspoon salt

2 teaspoons baking powder
8 teaspoons baking soda
1 cup milk
10 cups flour
2 cups whole wheat flour

Mix all ingredients well. Chill dough 8 hours or overnight. Shape into 1-inch balls. Roll in white sugar. Flatten slightly. Bake at 350 degrees for 8 to 10 minutes. Do not overbake. Cool completely before putting together sandwich-style with cream cheese filling. Yield: 115 sandwich cookies. These cookies store well in freezer for several months.

CREAM CHEESE FILLING:

½ cup butter, softened
1 (8 ounce) package cream cheese, softened
1 teaspoon vanilla

⅛ teaspoon salt
1 tablespoon milk
1 tablespoon flour
6 cups powdered sugar

Mix together until creamy.

Jolene Bontrager, Topeka, IN

Molasses Gingersnap Cookies

2 cups molasses
1 cup sugar
1 cup lard
1 cup buttermilk
2 eggs
1 teaspoon salt

4 teaspoons baking soda
1 teaspoon ground cloves
1½ teaspoons ginger
2 teaspoons cinnamon
½ teaspoon nutmeg
8 cups flour (approximate for soft dough)

Mix all ingredients. Drop by teaspoon on cookie sheet. Dip a glass in sugar and press dough. Bake at 375 degrees for 10 to 12 minutes.

This recipe is rather old-fashioned, but it is delicious. These cookies are just as good when they are a month old.

Mrs. Lavern Schrock, Marion, MI

Chewy Oat Bran Cookies

1½ cups butter
1 cup sugar
1 cup brown sugar
2 eggs
1 teaspoon baking soda
1 teaspoon vanilla

1 teaspoon salt
1 teaspoon cream of tartar
2½ cups quick oats
1 cup oat bran
2¼ cups flour
2¼ cups rice crisp cereal

Mix all together. Drop by spoonfuls onto cookie sheet. Bake at 350 degrees for 10 minutes.

Esta Hostetler, New Concord, OH

Butterscotch Delights

2 cups sugar
2 cups brown sugar
1 cup shortening
1 cup butter, softened
5 eggs
2 tablespoons vanilla
¼ cup milk

5 cups quick oats
3 teaspoons baking soda
2½ teaspoons baking powder
2 teaspoons salt
5 cups flour
Powdered sugar

Mix sugar, brown sugar, shortening, butter, eggs, and vanilla. Beat until fluffy. Then mix in milk and oats. Add baking soda, baking powder, salt, and flour; mix well. Shape into balls. Roll in powdered sugar and press down slightly on greased cookie sheets. Bake at 375 degrees for 10 minutes until light golden.

Phebe Peight, McVeytown, PA

Coconut Oatmeal Cookies

1¾ cups shortening
2 cups sugar
2 cups brown sugar
4 eggs, beaten
1 teaspoon salt

2 teaspoons baking powder
2 teaspoons vanilla
2 cups shredded coconut
1 cup chopped nuts (optional)
5 cups oats

Cream together shortening and sugars. Add eggs. Mix in salt, baking powder, vanilla, coconut, and nuts. Mix well. Add oats. Mix well. Form balls and place on cookie sheets. Flatten balls. Bake at 400 degrees for 10 minutes.

Fannie Bontrager, Sturgis, MI

Oatmeal Sandwich Cookies

1½ cups shortening
2½ cups brown sugar
4 eggs
2 teaspoons vanilla
2 teaspoons cinnamon

1½ teaspoons baking soda
1 teaspoon salt
½ teaspoon nutmeg
2¾ cups flour
4 cups quick oats

In large mixing bowl, cream shortening and brown sugar. Add eggs, one at a time, beating well after each. Add vanilla. Combine dry ingredients, except oats. Add to creamed mixture. Stir in oats. Bake at 350 degrees for 10 minutes. Cool. Pair 2 cookies with filling in between. Yield: 28 sandwich cookies.

Filling:

¾ cup shortening
2 egg whites, beaten stiff
1 (7 ounce) jar marshmallow crème

3 cups powdered sugar
1 tablespoon vanilla

Mix well.

Jolene Bontrager, Topeka, IN

Pumpkin Chocolate Chip Sandwich Cookies

1 cup butter, softened
¾ cup brown sugar
¾ cup sugar
1 egg, beaten
1 teaspoon vanilla
2 cups flour
1 cup quick oats
1 teaspoon baking soda
1 teaspoon cinnamon
1 cup pumpkin
1½ cups chocolate chips

Cream butter with sugars. Add egg and vanilla. Mix in flour, oats, baking soda, and cinnamon. Add pumpkin. Fold in chocolate chips. Form into balls or drop by spoonfuls onto cookie sheets. Bake at 350 degrees for 10 to 12 minutes. When cool, spread filling between 2 cookies. Yield: about 19 sandwich cookies.

Filling:

4 ounces cream cheese, softened
¼ cup butter, softened
¼ teaspoon vanilla
2 to 3 cups powdered sugar

Blend all until smooth.

Joann Miller, Mount Vernon, OH

Pumpkin Snickerdoodles

2 cups flour
½ teaspoon baking soda
½ teaspoon cream of tartar
½ teaspoon salt
⅛ teaspoon mace or nutmeg
½ cup butter, melted and
   cooled

1 cup sugar
½ cup pumpkin puree
1 large egg
1 teaspoon vanilla
⅓ cup sugar
1 teaspoon cinnamon
½ teaspoon allspice

Sift together flour, baking soda, cream of tartar, salt, and mace. In large bowl, whisk butter, 1 cup sugar, pumpkin, egg, and vanilla. Add flour mixture and stir about 2 minutes to combine. In small bowl, mix ⅓ cup sugar, cinnamon, and allspice. Drop spoonfuls of dough into sugar mixture and form into 1½-inch balls. Place on cookie sheets. Flatten to ½ inch. Sprinkle with more sugar mixture if desired. Bake at 350 degrees for 8 to 10 minutes.

Esther L. Miller, Fredericktown, OH

Raisin-Filled Cookies

2 cups shortening (can use half butter)
2 cups sugar
1 cup brown sugar
4 eggs

2 tablespoons milk
7 cups flour
2 teaspoons baking soda
1 teaspoon salt
2 teaspoons vanilla

Cream shortening and sugars. Beat eggs with milk and add to creamed mixture. Add dry ingredients and vanilla. Mix well. Shape into rolls, wrap in wax paper, and chill overnight.

Filling:

4 cups raisins
2 cups water
1 cup sugar
2 teaspoons vinegar

2 tablespoons flour
2 teaspoons vanilla
1 cup chopped nuts

Cook all ingredients together until raisins are soft. Cool.

Cut cookie dough into ⅛-inch slices. Place 1 tablespoon filling in middle of a dough slice and cover with another slice. As top cookie bakes, it will seal itself to bottom cookie. Bake at 350 degrees for 15 minutes until lightly browned.

These keep well in the freezer.

Velma Schrock, Goshen, IN

Wyoming Whopper Cookies

⅔ cup butter
¾ cup sugar
1¼ cups brown sugar
3 eggs, beaten
⅛ teaspoon salt

1½ cups chunky peanut butter
6 cups old-fashioned oats
2 teaspoons baking soda
12 ounces chocolate chips
1½ cups raisins (optional)

In large saucepan, melt butter over low heat. Blend in sugars, eggs, salt, and peanut butter. Mix until smooth. Add oats, baking soda, chocolate chips, and raisins. Dough will be sticky. (Note: Dough works best if you refrigerate it overnight before baking.) Drop by spoonfuls onto greased cookie sheets. Flatten slightly. Bake at 350 degrees for about 15 minutes. Remove to wire rack. Yield: 2 dozen.

These cookies don't take flour and are delicious!

Martha Petersheim, Junction City, OH

Almost Candy Bars

1½ cups flour
½ cup cocoa powder
¾ cup powdered sugar
1 cup butter

8 ounces chocolate chips
8 ounces butterscotch chips
1 cup shredded coconut
1 (14 ounce) can sweetened
   condensed milk

Mix together flour, cocoa powder, powdered sugar, and butter. Press into 9x13-inch pan. Sprinkle with chocolate chips, butterscotch chips, and coconut. Drizzle with milk. Bake at 350 degrees for 20 minutes.

Mrs. John H. Mullet, Cass City, MI

Apple Strudel Squares

⅔ cup scalded milk
1 cup butter
1 tablespoon yeast
⅓ cup warm water

3 teaspoons sugar
4 egg yolks
3½ cups flour
1 quart apple pie filling

Combine milk and butter until melted. Dissolve yeast in warm water. Combine yeast with milk. Add sugar, egg yolks, and flour. Mix to make soft dough. Divide dough in half. Roll half onto 11x16-inch cookie sheet. Spread with apple pie filling. Roll second half of dough into 11x16-inch rectangle. Cut in strips and arrange on top of pie filling in lattice style. Let rise 1 hour in warm place. Bake at 350 degrees for 30 to 45 minutes until top is golden brown. Drizzle with your favorite glaze or dust with doughnut sugar (similar to powdered sugar, but it will not melt as easily).

Kathryn Troyer, Rutherford, TN

Can't-Leave-Alone Bars

1 box yellow cake mix
2 eggs
3 cups vegetable oil

½ cup butter
1 cup chocolate chips
1 (14 ounce) can sweetened
condensed milk

Blend cake mix, eggs, and oil. Press into bottom of 9x13-inch pan, reserving ¾ cup for topping. Melt butter, chocolate chips, and milk together. Pour over crust. Pour small dabs of reserved crust over top. Bake at 350 degrees for 35 to 40 minutes.

Liz Miller, Decatur, TN

Caramel Chip Bars

½ cup butter
32 caramels
1 (14 ounce) can sweetened
  condensed milk
1 box yellow cake mix

½ cup vegetable oil
2 eggs
1 cup vanilla chips
2 cups mini chocolate chips
1 Heath candy bar, crushed

In saucepan, mix butter, caramels, and milk over low heat. In bowl, mix cake mix, oil, and eggs. Add vanilla and chocolate chips. Put three-quarters of batter in greased 9x13-inch pan. Bake at 350 degrees for 15 minutes. Let rest for 10 minutes. Pour caramel mixture over top. Spread with remaining batter. Bake 25 more minutes. Do not overbake. When done, sprinkle with candy pieces.

Emma Jo Hochstetler, Nappanee, IN

CHERRY CHEESE BARS

1 cup nuts, divided
1¼ cups flour
½ cup brown sugar
½ cup butter-flavored
   shortening
½ cup shredded coconut

1 (8 ounce) package cream
   cheese, softened
⅓ cup sugar
1 egg
1 teaspoon vanilla
1 (21 ounce) can cherry pie
   filling

Chop ½ cup nuts coarsely for topping. Set aside. Chop remaining ½ cup nuts finely. In bowl, combine flour and brown sugar. Cut in shortening until fine crumbs form. Add ½ cup finely chopped nuts and coconut. Mix well. Remove ½ cup dough crumbs. Set aside. Press remaining mixture into bottom of greased 9x13-inch pan. Bake at 350 degrees for 12 to 15 minutes until edges are lightly browned. In bowl, beat cream cheese, sugar, egg, and vanilla until smooth. Spread over hot baked crust. Return to oven. Bake 10 minutes. Spread cherry pie filling over top. Return to oven for 15 minutes. Cool. Yield: 24 bars.

Lizzie Schwartz, Berne, IN

Chocolate Oatmeal Bars

½ cup butter, softened
½ cup brown sugar
1 egg
1 teaspoon vanilla

½ cup flour
½ cup quick oats
1 cup semisweet chocolate chips
½ cup chopped pecans

In mixing bowl, cream butter and brown sugar. Beat in egg and vanilla. Add flour and oats; mix well. Pour into lightly greased 7x11-inch baking pan. Bake at 375 degrees for 15 to 20 minutes or until lightly browned. Cool on wire rack for 3 to 5 minutes. Sprinkle with chocolate chips. When melted, spread chocolate over bars. Top with nuts. Yield: 1½ dozen.

Martha Petersheim, Junction City, OH

Chocolate Revel Bars

1 cup butter
2 cups sugar
2 eggs
2 teaspoons vanilla

2½ cups flour
1 teaspoon salt
1 teaspoon baking soda
3 cups oats

In large bowl, cream butter with sugar. Add remaining ingredients. Spread two-thirds of batter in greased 9x13-inch pan. Top with filling. Spread remaining batter on top. Bake at 350 degrees for 25 to 30 minutes.

Filling:

12 ounces chocolate chips
1 (14 ounce) can sweetened condensed milk

2 tablespoons butter
½ teaspoon salt

In saucepan, melt ingredients together, stirring until smooth.

Betty Miller, Decatur, IN

CREAM CHEESE BARS

¼ cup sugar
¼ cup vegetable oil
1 egg
1 teaspoon salt

1 tablespoon yeast
1 cup warm water
1 cup doughnut mix
2½ to 3 cups flour

Mix sugar, oil, egg, salt, yeast, and water. Add in doughnut mix and flour. Knead until soft. Spread on greased 11.5x17-inch pan and let rise 30 minutes. Bake at 325 degrees for 15 to 20 minutes or until light brown. Cool.

FILLING:

1 cup cold milk
1 (3 ounce) box instant vanilla pudding mix

1 (8 ounce) package cream cheese, softened
1 (8 ounce) tub whipped topping

Removed baked bars from pan and cut in half lengthwise. Spread half with filling. Place other half on top. Frost with caramel frosting and dust with mixture of cinnamon and powdered sugar.

Jolene Bontrager, Topeka, IN

CREAM-FILLED DOUGHNUT BARS

1 cup lukewarm water
1 tablespoon yeast
¼ cup brown sugar
1 egg, beaten

¼ cup oil
1 teaspoon salt
1 cup doughnut mix
3 cups flour

Combine water and yeast; let stand until foamy. Add brown sugar, egg, oil, and salt; mix well. Add doughnut mix; mix well. Add flour 1 cup at a time, kneading well. Cover and let rise 1 hour, then punch down and roll out on large well-greased cookie sheet and let rise 1 hour. Bake at 350 degrees for 12 to 15 minutes. Cool completely, then cut in half lengthwise.

FILLING:

1 cup scalded milk
1 (3 ounce) box instant vanilla
   pudding mix

1 (8 ounce) package cream cheese
1 (8 ounce) tub whipped topping

Mix filling ingredients together and spread on bottom layer. Put top layer back on. Frost with your favorite caramel frosting and sprinkle with cinnamon and sugar.

These are delicious! When we get together for our family night, the girls often bring one pan of these. So good!

Lorene Herschberger, Sullivan, IL

Double Chocolate Crumble Bars

½ cup margarine
¾ cup sugar
2 eggs
1 teaspoon vanilla
¾ cup flour
2 tablespoons cocoa powder
1 teaspoon salt
½ teaspoon baking powder
½ cup nuts (optional)
2 cups small marshmallows
6 to 8 ounces chocolate chips
1 cup peanut butter
1½ cups rice crisp cereal

Mix first 9 ingredients in order. Spread on greased 9x13-inch pan. Bake at 350 degrees for 15 minutes. Remove from oven. Sprinkle with marshmallows. Return to oven for 3 minutes. In saucepan, melt chocolate chips with peanut butter. Stir in cereal. Spread over baked bar dough. Cool and cut.

Mrs. Sarah Gingerich, Howard, OH

Fruit Bars

1½ cups sugar
1 cup butter
4 eggs, beaten
1½ teaspoons vanilla
3 cups flour
½ teaspoon salt
1½ teaspoons baking powder
Pie filling

Cream sugar and butter. Add eggs and vanilla. Sift together flour, salt, and baking powder. Add to creamed mixture. Spread two-thirds of dough in large greased pan. Cover with your favorite pie filling. Spoon remaining batter on top. Bake at 350 degrees for 30 to 40 minutes. Glaze while still warm.

Glaze:

1½ cups powdered sugar
2 teaspoons melted butter
½ teaspoon vanilla
Milk

Mix all together with enough milk to reach desired thickness.

Mrs. Aaron (Emma) Gingerich, Bremen, OH

GRANOLA BARS

5 tablespoons butter
1 (10 ounce) bag mini
    marshmallows

3 cups granola
2 cups rice crisp cereal
1 cup white chocolate chips

In 6-quart pan, melt butter, then add marshmallows and stir to melt. Remove from heat. Add granola and cereal. Stir well. Press into well-buttered cookie sheet. Melt white chocolate and drizzle over all. Cut into bars before they cool.

GRANOLA:

1 (42 ounce) can quick oats
3 cups whole wheat flour
¾ tablespoon baking soda

½ teaspoon salt
¾ cup butter
1 cup maple syrup or honey

Mix oats, flour, baking soda, and salt. Melt butter and mix with maple syrup. Pour over dry ingredients. Mix well. Spread lightly on cookie sheets and dry in oven at 250 degrees for about 45 minutes or until dry. Stir occasionally.

These bars are very simple to make and a healthy snack for picnics. You can add raisins, nuts, or small chocolate chips to the bars. Also very good to eat with yogurt.

Mrs. Elizabeth Miller, Middlefield, OH

PUMPKIN PIE SQUARES

1 cup flour
½ cup quick oats
½ cup brown sugar
½ cup butter, softened
2 (15 ounce) cans pumpkin
    puree
2 (12 ounce) cans
    evaporated milk
4 eggs

1½ cups sugar
2 teaspoons cinnamon
1 teaspoon ginger
½ teaspoon ground cloves
1 teaspoon salt
½ cup brown sugar
½ cup chopped pecans
2 tablespoons butter, melted

Combine first 4 ingredients until crumbly; press into greased 9x13-inch pan. Bake at 350 degrees for 15 minutes. In mixing bowl, beat together pumpkin, milk, eggs, sugar, cinnamon, ginger, cloves, and salt until smooth. Pour over baked crust. Bake for 45 minutes. Combine ½ cup brown sugar, pecans, and 2 tablespoons butter into crumbs. Sprinkle over top and bake an additional 15 to 20 minutes until set. Cool. Store in refrigerator. Yield: 16 to 20 servings.

Jolene Bontrager, Topeka, IN

PINEAPPLE CREAM CHEESE SQUARES

20 ounces crushed pineapple,
    drained
2 eggs
2 cups sugar

1 teaspoon vanilla
2 teaspoons baking powder
2 cups flour

Mix together pineapple, eggs, and sugar. Add vanilla, baking powder, and flour. Spread on greased cookie sheet and bake at 350 degrees for 20 minutes. Cool. Frost.

FROSTING:

1 (8 ounce) package cream
    cheese, softened

½ cup butter, browned
2 cups powdered sugar

Blend together until smooth.

Edna Bontrager, Gladwin, MI

MONSTER BARS

1¼ cups brown sugar
1 cup sugar
¾ cup shortening
3 eggs
1½ cups peanut butter
1 tablespoon light corn syrup

2 teaspoons baking soda
1 teaspoon vanilla
4½ cups quick oats
1 cup flour
1 cup chocolate chips
1 cup M&Ms

In large bowl, combine sugars and shortening. Beat until well blended. Beat in eggs. Add peanut butter, corn syrup, baking soda, and vanilla. Mix well. Stir in oats and flour. Add chocolate chips and M&Ms. Spread in bar pan. Bake at 350 degrees for 11 to 13 minutes or until just beginning to brown.

Vera Mast, Kalona, IA

PEANUT BUTTER BARS

1½ cups flour
2 teaspoons baking powder
½ teaspoon salt
1 cup creamy peanut butter
½ cup butter

2 cups firmly packed
  brown sugar
6 eggs
¾ cup milk
2 teaspoons vanilla

Mix flour, baking powder, and salt. In larger bowl, with mixer on medium speed, beat peanut butter, butter, and brown sugar until light and fluffy. Add eggs, one at a time, beating after each. Add milk and vanilla; mix well. Pour batter into large greased cookie sheet and bake at 350 degrees for 20 minutes or until done. Cool and frost.

PEANUT BUTTER FROSTING:

½ cup creamy peanut butter
5 to 6 tablespoons milk

2 cups powdered sugar
1 teaspoon vanilla

Mix together until fluffy.

A yummy cake-like bar that is easy to take to a friend's house for coffee break.

Anita Lorraine Petersheim, Fredericktown, OH

RHUBARB CUSTARD BARS

CRUST:

1½ cups flour   ⅛ teaspoon salt
½ cup sugar   9 tablespoons butter, chilled

In mixing bowl, combine flour, sugar, and salt. Cut in butter until mixture resembles coarse meal. Press mixture in greased 9x13-inch baking dish. Bake at 350 degrees for 15 minutes, until crust is golden brown.

FILLING:

⅓ cup flour   3 eggs
1½ cups sugar   5 cups chopped rhubarb
1½ cups milk

In large bowl, combine flour and sugar. Add milk and eggs, stirring until well blended. Stir in rhubarb. Pour mixture over crust. Bake at 350 degrees for 40 minutes or until set. Cool.

TOPPING:

½ cup sugar   ½ teaspoon vanilla
1 (8 ounce) package cream   1 cup whipped topping
  cheese

In mixing bowl, beat together sugar, cream cheese, and vanilla at medium speed until smooth. Gently fold in whipped topping. Spread evenly over baked rhubarb. Cover and chill at least 1 hour.

Note: To make a bar with a thinner amount of filling, mix a 1½ batch of crust and spread into a jelly roll pan. Proceed as directed above.

Diana Miller, Fredericktown, OH

Swiss Roll Bars

1 box cake mix
1 (8 ounce) package cream
  cheese, softened
1½ cups powdered sugar
2 tablespoons milk

1 (8 ounce) tub whipped
  topping
5 tablespoons butter
1½ cups milk chocolate chips

Mix cake according to package directions. Bake on prepared cookie or jelly roll sheet. Blend cream cheese, sugar, and milk. Add whipped topping. Spread over cooked cake. Chill. Melt butter gently and add chocolate chips, stirring until smooth. Spread over cream cheese layer. Chill.

This recipe is used a lot for Sunday night youth singings.

Mary K. Bontrager, Middlebury, IN

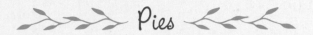

Pies

FRIED PIES

9 cups flour	3 cups shortening
2 tablespoons sugar	2 cups water
1 tablespoon salt	Thick pie filling

Combine flour, sugar, and salt. Cut in shortening. Slowly add water. Mix together like you would pie dough. Roll balls of dough into 7-inch circles. Put ½ cup pie filling in middle of each circle. Moisten edges. Fold circle in half and crimp edges together with fork. Deep-fry pies in oil at 350 degrees until golden brown. Cool and glaze.

GLAZE:

6 cups powdered sugar	1 cup warm water
1 package gelatin or 3 tablespoons cornstarch	

Mix all together until smooth.

Ida R. Schwartz, Salem, IN

BLACK RASPBERRY CREAM PIE

1 cup sour cream	2 (9-inch) unbaked pie shells
1 (8 ounce) package cream cheese, softened	Black raspberry pie filling
2 cups sugar, divided	½ cup butter
	2 cups flour

Mix sour cream, cream cheese, and 1 cup sugar. Spread in bottom of pie shells. Top with raspberry pie filling. Mix together butter, flour, and 1 cup sugar to form crumbs. Divide and sprinkle over both pies. Bake at 350 degrees until crumbs are golden brown.

Jolene Bontrager, Topeka, IN

GLAZED CHERRY FRIED PIES

4 cups flour	1½ teaspoons salt
1 cup shortening	½ cup milk
1 teaspoon baking powder	1 quart cherry pie filling

Mix flour, shortening, baking powder, salt, and milk to form dough. Roll dough out on lightly floured surface. Cut dough in small rounds. Spoon 2 tablespoons pie filling in center of each round. Fold in half to close. Seal edges. Heat 2½ inches oil in pan to 350 to 375 degrees. Deep-fry pies for 3 minutes each.

GLAZE:

2 teaspoons light corn syrup	1½ cups powdered sugar
1 teaspoon vanilla	2 to 3 tablespoons hot water

Mix all together and brush over fried pies.

Lovina N. Borntrager, Clark, MO

BUTTER PECAN PUMPKIN PIE

1 quart butter pecan ice cream, softened	¼ teaspoon nutmeg
1 (9 inch) baked pie shell	1 cup heavy whipping cream, whipped
1 cup pumpkin puree	½ cup caramel ice cream topping
½ cup sugar	½ cup chocolate ice cream topping
¼ teaspoon cinnamon	Whipped topping
¼ teaspoon ginger	

Spread ice cream into pie shell. Freeze for 2 hours until firm. In small bowl, combine pumpkin, sugar, and spices. Fold in whipped cream. Spread over ice cream. Cover and freeze for 2 hours or until firm. (This may be frozen for up to 2 months.) Remove from freezer 15 minutes before slicing. Drizzle with toppings and add dollops of whipped topping.

Jean Hochstetler, Pearisburg, VA

Cappuccino Pie

- 1½ cups chocolate chips
- 1 tablespoon corn syrup
- 3 graham cracker piecrusts
- 1 (8 ounce) package cream cheese
- ¾ cup powdered sugar
- 2 (3 ounce) boxes instant chocolate pudding mix
- 2 cups milk
- ½ cup instant coffee
- ½ cup cappuccino mix
- 1 cup hot water
- 1 (16 ounce) tub whipped topping

Melt chocolate chips and corn syrup. Pour into bottom of piecrusts. In bowl, blend cream cheese and powdered sugar. In separate bowl, mix pudding mixes with milk. In another bowl, dissolve coffee and cappuccino mix in hot water. Combine cream cheese, pudding, and coffee mixtures. Fill pies. Top with whipped topping. Garnish with shredded chocolate or chocolate chips if desired.

Serve this with coffee. It is a chocolate lover's pie. Great for dinners, cookouts, and more.

Daniel and Fannie Miller, New Concord, OH

Coconut Oatmeal Pie

6 eggs, separated
1 cup corn syrup
1 teaspoon maple flavoring
½ cup brown sugar
4 tablespoons flour
5 tablespoons melted butter

4 cups hot milk
1 cup oatmeal
1 cup shredded coconut
1 teaspoon salt
2 (9 inch) unbaked pie shells

Beat egg whites until stiff. Set aside. In bowl, combine corn syrup with maple flavoring. Add brown sugar and flour. Mix. Add egg yolks, butter, and milk. Mix. Stir in oats, coconut, and salt. Then add egg whites. Pour into pie shells. Bake at 375 degrees for 1 hour until set.

Katie Hershberger, Freeport, OH

Mom's "Ice Cream" Pie

¾ cup sugar
¼ cup brown sugar
1 rounded tablespoon flour
¾ teaspoon cinnamon
2 eggs, separated

1 cup heavy whipping cream
1 cup milk
½ teaspoon vanilla
1 (9 inch) unbaked pie shell

In bowl, mix sugars, flour, cinnamon, and egg yolks. Slowly mix in cream, milk, and vanilla. In separate bowl, beat egg whites until stiff. Fold into first mixture until incorporated. Pour into pie shell. Bake at 375 degrees for 10 minutes. Reduce heat to 325 degrees and continue baking for 25 minutes or until knife inserted near center comes out clean.

This recipe is seventy-five years old.

Ella Arlene Yoder, Arcola, IL

Lemon Blossom Pie

3 cups water	½ cup cornstarch
½ teaspoon salt	4 tablespoons butter, melted
6 egg yolks, beaten	½ cup lemon juice
2 cups sugar	3 (9-inch) baked pie shells

In saucepan, boil water and salt. In bowl, mix egg yolks, sugar, cornstarch, butter, and lemon juice until smooth. Slowly add to boiling water. Cook until thick. Pour hot filling into baked shells.

MERINGUE:

6 egg whites	½ cup sugar

Beat egg whites until stiff peaks form. Add sugar and beat well. Spread over pies. Brown meringue in oven at 350 degrees until golden brown, approximately 10 to 15 minutes.

VARIATIONS:

¾ teaspoon lemon flavoring may be added to filling
½ teaspoon cream of tartar may be added to meringue

Ida R. Schwartz, Salem, TN

Sour Cream Apple Pie

¾ cup sugar	1 egg
1 cup sour cream	¼ teaspoon salt
½ teaspoon vanilla	3 cups sliced apples
2 tablespoons flour	1 (9-inch) unbaked pie shell

Mix sugar, sour cream, vanilla, flour, egg, and salt. Add apples. Pour into pie shell. Top with crumbs. Bake at 400 degrees for 15 minutes. Reduce heat to 350 degrees and bake 25 to 30 minutes.

Crumbs:

¼ cup butter	⅔ cup flour
⅓ cup sugar	½ teaspoon cinnamon

Mix together.

Mattie Petersheim, Junction City, OH

SOUR CREAM PUMPKIN PIES

1 (15 ounce) can pumpkin
1 (14 ounce) can sweetened
  condensed milk
2 teaspoons pumpkin pie
  spice
½ teaspoon ginger (optional)
½ teaspoon nutmeg (optional)
2 eggs, beaten
½ teaspoon salt
2 (9-inch) unbaked pie shells
½ cup nuts, minced (optional)

Combine pumpkin, milk, spices, eggs, and salt; mix well. Divide into pie shells and bake at 425 degrees for 15 minutes. Reduce heat to 350 degrees and bake 20 minutes longer. Top with sour cream topping and crumbs. Garnish with nuts. Bake another 15 minutes.

TOPPING:

1 (8 ounce) package cream
  cheese, softened
¾ cup sugar
1½ cups sour cream

Cream together cream cheese and sugar. Mix in sour cream until smooth.

CRUMBS:

1 cup brown sugar
1 cup flour
6 tablespoons butter, softened

Combine ingredients into crumbly mixture.

Edna Miller, Apple Creek, OH

STRAWBERRY RHUBARB PIE

3 cups rhubarb
1 cup fresh strawberries,
  sliced
1 (9-inch) unbaked pie shell
  and top
2 eggs
1½ cups sugar
3 tablespoons flour
Dash salt

Mix rhubarb and strawberries. Put into pie shell. In bowl, beat eggs, sugar, flour, and salt. Pour over fruit. Top with crust. Bake at 350 degrees for 1 hour until browned and bubbly.

Mrs. Ray Hershberger, Scottville, MI

Vanilla Crumb Pie

1 cup brown sugar	½ teaspoon cream of tartar
1 cup corn syrup	1 teaspoon vanilla
2 cups water	1 teaspoon baking soda
2 tablespoons flour	3 (9-inch) unbaked pie shells
1 egg	

In saucepan, boil together brown sugar, corn syrup, water, and flour for 1 minute. Set aside. In large bowl, beat egg, cream of tartar, vanilla, and baking soda. Add to syrup. Divide mixture equally between pie shells. Top with crumb topping. Bake at 350 to 375 degrees for 45 minutes.

Crumb Topping:

2 cups pastry flour	½ teaspoon baking soda
1 cup brown sugar	1 teaspoon cream of tartar
½ cup lard	

Mix together until crumbly.

Mrs. Samuel J. Schwartz, Bryant, IN

"Thank You" Pie Filling

½ cup sugar	⅓ cup clear-jel
1 cup water	½ cup water
¼ teaspoon salt	½ cup light corn syrup
½ teaspoon lemon juice	2 heaping cups chopped raw fruit

Heat sugar, 1 cup water, salt, and lemon juice. In small bowl, make a paste of clear-jel and ½ cup water. Stir into heated mixture and bring to a boil. It will get very thick. Remove from heat. Add corn syrup and fruit. Fill quart jar, and cold pack for 20 minutes. Give jar as thank-you gift or fill baked pie shell, top with whipped cream, and share with someone.

Tips: For sour cherries, use ¾ cup sugar and add 1 teaspoon red food coloring. For apples, add 1 teaspoon apple pie spice.

Betty Miller, Decatur, IN

Chocolate Piecrust

1¼ cups flour
½ teaspoon salt
⅓ cup sugar
¼ cup cocoa powder

½ cup shortening
½ teaspoon vanilla
2 to 3 tablespoons cold water

Sift flour, salt, sugar, and cocoa powder together. Cut in shortening. Add vanilla. Sprinkle with cold water. Form into ball. Roll out and put in pie pan. Also bake trimmings to crumble for topping. Can be baked and filled with instant vanilla pudding. Or fill with something like pecan pie filling, butterscotch, or custard and bake.

Mary Miller, Junction City, OH

Piecrust

3 cups sifted flour
1 cup shortening
½ teaspoon salt

1 egg
⅓ cup water
1 teaspoon vinegar

Mix flour, shortening, and salt. Beat egg; add water and vinegar. Add to flour mixture. Yield: 2 9-inch double crust pies or about 4 single crusts.

Tip: Before baking piecrusts, spritz with water to keep them from creeping down in pan.

Iva Yoder, Goshen, IN

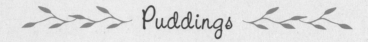

Puddings

COFFEE PUDDING

1½ quarts milk
1 cup sugar
3 teaspoons instant coffee
1 cup clear-jel

1 tablespoon vanilla
1 tablespoon butter
1 (8 ounce) tub whipped
  topping

Bring milk and sugar to a boil. Do not stir. Whisk in instant coffee and clear-jel. Turn heat off and add vanilla and butter. Cool; do not stir while cooling. After it's cooled, add whipped topping.

Mattie Petersheim, Junction City, OH

COTTAGE CHEESE PUDDING

24 ounces cottage cheese
1 (3 ounce) box orange gelatin
1 (8 ounce) tub whipped
  topping

1 can fruit, drained (oranges,
  peaches, pineapple,
  or your choice)

Stir together cottage cheese and gelatin. Stir in whipped topping. Fold in fruit.

Ada Mast, Kalona, IA

CORNSTARCH PUDDING

2 quarts milk	**3 eggs**
½ cup cornstarch	**1 teaspoon vanilla**
1¼ cups sugar	

In saucepan, heat milk to a boil. Remove 1 cup and mix with cornstarch, sugar, and eggs using beater. Pour into saucepan of hot milk, stirring constantly. Cook until thick. Remove from heat and add vanilla. After pudding is cooled, you may add some whipped topping and crushed Oreo cookies. Or layer in glass bowl with crushed cookies or graham cracker crumbs.

Anna M. Byler, Clymer, PA

GRAHAM CRACKER PUDDING

24 graham crackers, crushed
½ cup butter, melted
⅓ cup brown sugar
2 cups milk
½ cup sugar

2 egg yolks
2 heaping tablespoons flour
½ teaspoon salt
1 teaspoon vanilla
1 cup whipped topping

Combine crackers, butter, and brown sugar. Set aside. In saucepan, bring milk, sugar, egg yolks, flour, and salt to a slow boil over medium heat. Cook until thickened. Add vanilla. Cool. When cool, fold in whipped topping. In glass serving bowl, layer pudding then crumbs. Alternate layers, leaving some crumbs for top. Banana slices can also be added to layers.

Mrs. Orie Detweiler, Inola, OK

MAPLE SPUNCH PUDDING

1½ packages gelatin
¼ cup cold water
2 cups boiling water
2 cups brown sugar
1 teaspoon maple flavoring
Pinch salt
5 tablespoons cornstarch
2 eggs, beaten

1½ cups sugar
½ teaspoon salt
½ teaspoon maple flavoring
5 cups milk
1 cup whipped topping
1 cup mini marshmallows
½ cup chopped walnuts or
    pecans

Soak gelatin in cold water. Add boiling water, brown sugar, 1 teaspoon maple flavoring, and a pinch of salt. Put in square pan, chill, then cut in cubes. In bowl, mix cornstarch, eggs, sugar, ½ teaspoon salt, and ½ teaspoon maple flavoring to make a paste. In saucepan, heat milk to boiling. Slowly add paste to boiling milk and whisk until smooth. Cool. When cold, add whipped topping, marshmallows, nuts, and gelatin cubes.

Mrs. Levi J. Stutzman, West Salem, OH

SWEETHEART PUDDING

PUDDING:

6 egg yolks
8 cups milk
2¼ cups sugar

1 teaspoon vanilla
6 tablespoons flour
6 tablespoons cornstarch

In saucepan, beat egg yolks. Add milk, sugar, and vanilla. In bowl, mix together flour and cornstarch. Add to first mixture and cook until thick. Cool.

CRUST:

3 cups graham cracker
    crumbs

½ cup butter, melted
¼ cup sugar

Mix crumbs with butter and sugar. Press in 9x13-inch pan, reserving some crumbs for topping. Pour pudding on top of crust.

TOPPING:

6 egg whites
3 tablespoons sugar

1 teaspoon vanilla

Beat egg whites, sugar, and vanilla until stiff and glossy. Layer on pudding and top with reserved crumbs. Bake at 350 degrees until nicely browned. Chill before serving.

Esther N. Borntrager, Clark, MO

Tapioca Pudding

2 quarts milk
1 cup tapioca
¾ cup sugar
1 cup brown sugar
2 rounded tablespoons
  cornstarch

2 eggs, beaten
1 (20 ounce) can crushed
  pineapple, drained
2 or 3 candy bars, chopped
Whipped topping

In large saucepan, heat milk to boiling; add tapioca. Cook on low heat until clear. In bowl, mix sugars, cornstarch, and eggs. Add a couple of spoonfuls of hot tapioca and mix well. Add to pan of tapioca and stir until it thickens. Cool. When tapioca pudding is cold, add pineapple and candy. If pudding is too thick, thin by mixing in whipped topping.

Fannie Bontrager, Sturgis, MI

Mocha Tapioca

6 cups water
1 teaspoon salt
1½ cups tapioca
2 cups brown sugar
2 eggs, beaten
¼ cup cornstarch

1 cup milk
1 cup sugar
¼ cup cocoa powder
2 tablespoons instant coffee
24 ounces whipped topping
Mini chocolate chips or toffee bits (optional)

In saucepan, combine water, salt, and tapioca. Cook until tapioca is clear, stirring frequently. Add brown sugar. In bowl, mix eggs, cornstarch, milk, sugar, cocoa powder, and instant coffee. Stir mixture into tapioca. Bring to a boil. Remove from heat and cool. Mix in whipped topping and chocolate chips.

Mrs. Lavern Schrock, Marion, MI

Upside-Down Date Pudding

1 cup chopped dates
1 cup boiling water
½ cup sugar
½ cup brown sugar
1 egg
2 tablespoons butter, melted

1 teaspoon salt
½ teaspoon baking powder
1 teaspoon baking soda
1½ cups flour
1 cup chopped nuts
Whipped topping

Mix dates with boiling water; let cool. Blend sugars, egg, and butter. Add salt, baking powder, baking soda, and flour. Stir in nuts and dates. Pour into greased 7x11-inch baking dish. Top with sauce. Bake at 350 degrees for 45 minutes. When cold, cut into squares and invert onto serving plates. Serve with dollop of whipped topping.

Sauce:

1½ cups brown sugar
1½ cups boiling water

1 tablespoon butter

Stir together until sugar and butter melt.

Mrs. Ivan Yoder, Junction City, OH

Other Desserts

FUDGE

2 cups sugar
6 tablespoons cocoa powder
⅔ cup milk

2 tablespoons corn syrup
4 tablespoons peanut butter
½ teaspoon vanilla

Cook sugar, cocoa powder, milk, and corn syrup to soft ball stage. Add peanut butter and vanilla. Spread in pan. Cool.

Lizzie Schwartz, Berne, IN

MOUNDS BALLS

1 cup butter
2 cups powdered sugar
2 cups shredded coconut
½ can (7 ounces) sweetened
   condensed milk

1 teaspoon vanilla
1 cup chopped walnuts
   (optional)
Chocolate for coating

Cream together butter and powdered sugar. Add coconut, milk, vanilla, and nuts. Stir until blended. Roll into balls and chill for 1 day. Dip into melted chocolate.

We also make these into bars. Create a graham cracker crust, spread the ball mixture onto crust, and top with a thin layer of melted chocolate. A doubled recipe fills a 9x13-inch pan.

Rebecca Schmidt, Carlisle, KY

CRUNCHY PEANUT BUTTER TREATS

3 cups peanut butter	5 cups rice crisp cereal
1 cup butter	2 cups powdered sugar
1 cup brown sugar	1½ cups chocolate chips
1 teaspoon vanilla	3 tablespoons butter

Mix together peanut butter, 1 cup butter, brown sugar, vanilla, and cereal. Add powdered sugar. Press into jelly roll pan. Chill. Melt together chocolate chips and 3 tablespoons butter. Spread over chilled mixture.

Katie Miller, Arthur, IL

BERRY CROISSANTS

1 (8 ounce) package cream
  cheese
½ cup powdered sugar
1 (8 ounce) tub whipped
  topping
½ cup raspberry yogurt

12 croissant rolls,
  sliced in half
Fresh strawberries, sliced
Fresh blueberries
Powdered sugar for dusting

Beat cream cheese and powdered sugar until smooth. Beat in whipped topping and yogurt. Chill until ready to use. Remove tops of rolls. Divide filling among rolls. Pile with fresh berries. Replace tops and dust with powdered sugar.

Kathryn Troyer, Rutherford, TN

PEANUT BUTTER CUPS

1 cup graham cracker
  crumbs
½ cup margarine
2 cups powdered sugar
1 cup peanut butter

½ cup sugar
2 tablespoons milk
2 tablespoons margarine
1 cup chocolate chips

Mix together cracker crumbs, ½ cup margarine, powdered sugar, and peanut butter. Put in 9x13-inch pan. In saucepan, bring sugar, milk, and 2 tablespoons margarine to a boil. Remove from heat and stir in chocolate chips until melted. Spread on crust. Chill and cut.

Lizzie Schwartz, Berne, IN

PORCUPINE BALLS

1 package large
  marshmallows
1 tablespoon butter
1 pound caramels

1 can condensed milk
Rice crisp cereal
Semisweet chocolate chips or
  chocolate candy coating

Remove marshmallows from package and place in freezer. In top of double broiler, melt butter and caramels with milk. Dip cold marshmallows in hot caramel mixture and then roll in cereal one at a time. Cool. Dip in melted chocolate.

We like to pile these on a nice glass platter and take them to the Christmas school program.

Mary Ellen Wengerd, Campbellsville, KY

CREAMY LIME PINEAPPLE DESSERT

1 (3 ounce) box lime gelatin
1 cup water
1 (8 ounce) package cream
  cheese

1 (16 ounce) can crushed
  pineapple (do not drain)
1 (8 ounce) tub whipped
  topping

Combine gelatin, water, and cream cheese in saucepan. Cover over low heat until thickened and cream cheese blends in. Cool before folding in pineapple and whipped topping. Pour into 9x13-inch pan and refrigerate until firm.

Jolene Bontrager, Topeka, IN

Brown Sugar Dumplings

1 cup brown sugar
2 cups hot water
2 tablespoons butter
½ cup nuts or raisins
½ cup sugar

1 cup flour
2 teaspoons baking powder
1 teaspoon vanilla
½ cup water or milk

In saucepan, mix brown sugar, hot water, and butter; bring to a boil. Add nuts. In bowl, mix sugar, flour, and baking powder until crumbly. Add vanilla and water, stirring until smooth. Pour hot syrup in 9x13-inch pan. Drop batter by spoonfuls onto syrup. Bake at 350 degrees for 30 to 40 minutes. Before serving, break into small pieces. Serve with ice cream or whipped cream.

Lydiann Yoder, Andover, OH

Chocolate Angel Pizza

1 cup flour
½ cup butter or margarine
¾ cup chopped nuts
2 teaspoons sugar
1 (3 ounce) box instant
chocolate pudding mix
1 (3 ounce) box instant vanilla
pudding mix

3 cups milk
1 (8 ounce) package cream
cheese, softened
1 cup sugar
6 ounces whipped topping
¼ cup chopped nuts

Mix flour, butter, ¾ cup nuts, and 2 teaspoons sugar. Press into 9x13-inch pan. Bake at 350 degrees for 25 minutes or until browned. Cool. In bowl, combine pudding mixes and mix with milk. Set aside. Blend cream cheese with 1 cup sugar. Add whipped topping. Spread half of cream mixture over cooled crust. Top with pudding mixture. Top with remaining cream mixture. Sprinkle with ¼ cup nuts. Cool.

Emma Schwartz, Berne, IN

Mini Key Lime Tarts

1 cup graham cracker
    crumbs
3 tablespoons butter, melted
2 egg yolks

½ can (7 ounces) sweetened
    condensed milk
3 tablespoons key lime juice

Mix cracker crumbs with butter. Press into bottom of paper-lined mini-muffin cups. Combine egg yolks, milk, and juice. Mix well and spoon over crust. Bake at 350 degrees for 10 minutes. Cool 10 minutes. Remove from pan. Refrigerate for a few hours, then remove liners before serving.

Eva Hochstetler, Dundee, OH

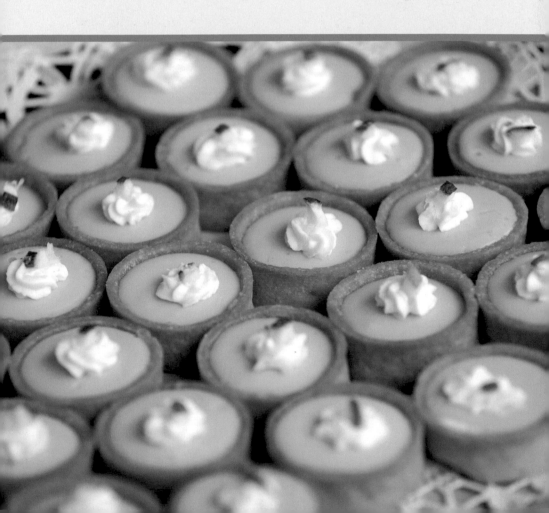

MESSY PINK STUFF

1 (8 ounce) package cream cheese, softened
1 (14 ounce) can sweetened condensed milk
1 (8 ounce) tub whipped topping

1 can cherry pie filling
1 (20 ounce) can crushed pineapple, drained

Beat cream cheese until smooth then add milk. Fold in whipped topping, pie filling, and pineapple. Chill thoroughly.

Betty Miller, Decatur, IN

STRAWBERRY DESSERT

1 (8 ounce) package cream cheese, softened
¾ cup sugar
1 (16 ounce) tub whipped topping

10 ounces strawberries
1 large can pineapple tidbits, drained

Mix all together and freeze.

A delicious snack for a warm day.

Joann Miller, Mount Vernon, OH

FROZEN PEANUT BUTTER DESSERT

1 sleeve graham crackers, crushed
4 tablespoons brown sugar
¼ cup melted butter
1 (8 ounce) package cream cheese, softened

⅔ cup peanut butter
2 cups powdered sugar
1 cup milk
6 cups whipped topping

Mix crackers, brown sugar, and butter. Reserve ½ cup for garnish. Press into 9x13-inch pan. Blend cream cheese, peanut butter, and powdered sugar until smooth. Add milk in small amounts, mixing well. Fold in whipped topping. Pour over crust. Sprinkle with reserved crumbs. Freeze. Thaw just before serving.

Mrs. Robert (Shirley) Schlabach, Crofton, KY

Éclair Dessert

1 cup water	1 cup flour
½ cup butter	4 eggs

Bring water and butter to a boil. Remove from heat. Stir in flour. Add eggs, beating after each one. Spread in greased jelly roll pan. Bake at 400 degrees for 25 minutes.

TOPPING:

3 cups milk	1 cup powdered sugar
1 cup instant vanilla pudding mix	1 (16 ounce) tub whipped topping
1 (8 ounce) package cream cheese	Chocolate syrup or pie filling

Beat together milk and pudding mix. In separate bowl, beat together cream cheese and powdered sugar. Blend both mixtures together and spread on crust. Spread whipped topping over top. Drizzle with your choice of chocolate syrup or pie filling. Our family favorite is fresh strawberry pie filling.

Miriam Raber, Flat Rock, IL

CREAMY FROZEN PINEAPPLE DESSERT

BUTTER CRUNCH CRUST:

½ cup butter, softened
1 cup flour

1 cup chopped pecans
¼ cup brown sugar

Mix together with fork to make crumbs. Spread loosely in 9x13-inch pan and bake at 350 degrees for 15 to 20 minutes just until light golden brown. Remove from oven and stir with spoon. Let cool. Stir again to make coarse crumbs. Set aside to cool completely. Spread in bottom of 9x13-inch serving dish, reserving ½ cup crumbs for topping.

FILLING:

1 cup sugar
1 (20 ounce) can crushed pineapple
1 (3 ounce) box orange gelatin
1 (3 ounce) box pineapple gelatin

2 (8 ounce) packages cream cheese, softened
1 (8 ounce) tub whipped topping

Combine sugar, pineapple, and gelatin in saucepan. Bring to a boil, stirring constantly until gelatin is dissolved. Remove from heat and cool. In bowl, beat cream cheese until smooth. Slowly add cooled gelatin mixture in small amounts. Beat until smooth. Fold in whipped topping. Spread over cooled crumb crust. Sprinkle with reserved crumbs. Freeze overnight. Remove from freezer 30 minutes before serving.

Kathryn Troyer, Rutherford, TN

Frozen Mocha Dessert

1 package Oreo cookies, crushed
¼ cup butter
1 (14 ounce) can sweetened condensed milk
1 (8 ounce) package cream cheese, softened
1 (16 ounce) tub whipped topping
½ cup chocolate syrup
2 to 4 teaspoons instant coffee, dissolved in 1 tablespoon hot water

Mix cookies with butter. Reserve about ⅔ cup. Press into 9x13-inch pan. Mix remaining ingredients and spread over crumb bottom. Top with reserved crumbs. Freeze.

Edna Miller, Apple Creek, OH

Mocha Brownie Dessert

CRUST:

1 box devil's food cake mix
¼ cup milk
½ cup butter, melted
1 egg
¾ cup chopped pecans (optional)

Mix all together and put in greased 9x13-inch pan. Bake at 350 degrees for 20 to 25 minutes. Cool.

FILLING:

12 ounces cream cheese
1 (14 ounce) can sweetened condensed milk
½ cup chocolate syrup
1 tablespoon instant coffee
1 tablespoon hot water
1 (16 ounce) tub whipped topping, divided
Chocolate curls (optional)
Chocolate-covered coffee beans (optional)

Beat cream cheese, gradually adding milk and syrup. Dissolve instant coffee in hot water and mix into first mixture. Blend well. Fold in 12 ounces whipped topping. Pour over crust. Freeze at least 5 hours before serving. Top with remaining whipped topping and garnish with chocolate curls or coffee beans.

Anita Lorraine Petersheim, Fredericktown, OH

Georgia Peaches and Cream

2 cups flour
¾ cup melted butter
1 cup chopped pecans
1¾ cups powdered sugar
1 (8 ounce) package cream cheese, softened
1 (12 ounce) tub whipped topping or 1½ cups whipped cream

1 cup sugar
3 tablespoons cornstarch
1 cup water
1 (3 ounce) box peach gelatin
4 cups peeled and sliced fresh peaches

In medium bowl, combine flour and butter. Stir in pecans. Press into 9x13-inch baking dish. Bake at 350 degrees for 10 minutes or until lightly browned. Cool completely. Mix powdered sugar with cream cheese until smooth. Fold in whipped topping. Spoon on top of crust, pushing sides up to make a slight well for peaches. Set aside. In medium saucepan, mix sugar and cornstarch. Over medium heat, slowly stir in water. Bring to a boil, stirring constantly, and cook 1 minute until mixture is bubbly, clear, and slightly thickened. Remove from heat and stir in peach gelatin. Heat until bubbly. Reserve ⅓ cup glaze for peaches. Spoon remaining glaze over cream mixture, leaving 1-inch border of cream visible. Stir reserved glaze into peaches and spoon peaches over glaze. Refrigerate several hours or overnight. Yield: 16 servings.

Ruby Miller, Auburn, KY

PEACH INTRIGUE

Peaches, sliced
¼ cup sugar
½ cup sour cream
½ teaspoon baking soda

½ cup brown sugar
¼ teaspoon salt
1 cup flour

Cover bottom of greased 9x13-inch pan with peaches. Sprinkle with sugar. Mix together sour cream, baking soda, brown sugar, salt, and flour. Spread or drop dough over peaches. Bake at 350 degrees for 45 minutes.

Tip: Other fruits will also work. If you add water or juice to the fruit, then add 2 tablespoons minute tapioca to the fruit layer to thicken the liquid.

Edna Miller, Junction City, OH

PINEAPPLE DESSERT

1 (14 ounce) can sweetened
   condensed milk
Graham crackers
Pineapple rings

Whipped topping
Maraschino cherries
   (optional)

Place unopened can of milk in pan of water and cook over low heat for 3 hours and 15 minutes. Cool. Cut off both ends of can and slide out jelled milk. Slice into equal-size rings. Place 1 graham cracker square on dessert plate. Top with 1 slice jelled milk and 1 ring pineapple. Garnish with dollop of whipped topping and 1 cherry. Repeat for each dessert serving.

Sarah Hershberger, McKenzie, TN

TRIPLE TREAT TORTE

CRUST:

½ cup butter
1 cup flour

⅔ cup chopped walnuts

Mix together and press crust into 9x13-inch pan. Bake at 350 degrees for 16 to 20 minutes. Cool.

FILLING:

1 cup powdered sugar
1 (8 ounce) package cream cheese, softened

½ cup peanut butter
1 (8 ounce) tub whipped topping

Mix well. Spread over crust.

TOPPING:

1 (3 ounce) box instant chocolate pudding mix
1 (3 ounce) box instant vanilla pudding mix

2¾ cups cold milk
1 (8 ounce) tub whipped topping

Combine pudding mixes and milk; mix well. Spread over filling. Top with whipped topping.

Betty Miller, Decatur, IN

PINEAPPLE PRETZEL FLUFF

1 cup coarsely crushed pretzels
½ cup butter, melted
1 cup sugar, divided
1 (8 ounce) package cream cheese, softened

1 (20 ounce) can crushed pineapple, drained
1 (12 ounce) tub frozen whipped topping, thawed

In bowl, combine pretzels, butter, and ½ cup sugar. Press into 9x13-inch baking pan. Bake at 400 degrees for 7 minutes. Cool. Meanwhile, in a mixing bowl, beat cream cheese and remaining sugar until creamy. Fold in pineapple and whipped topping. Chill until serving. Just before serving, break pretzel mixture into small pieces; stir into pineapple mixture.

Mrs. Ivan Yoder, Junction City, OH

TIRAMISU

2 (3 ounce) boxes instant
  vanilla pudding mix
4 cups cold milk
½ cup instant coffee
1 to 2 tablespoons hot water

2 (8 ounce) tubs whipped
  topping, divided
6 cups 1-inch brownie cubes
1 cup Oreo cookie crumbs
Cinnamon
Shaved chocolate

Mix pudding mixes with milk. Dissolve instant coffee with hot water; add to pudding. Fold in 1½ tubs whipped topping. Layer in glass bowl in following order: 3 cups brownie cubes, 2½ cups pudding mixture, ½ cup cookie crumbs. Repeat layers. Spread top with remaining whipped topping. Sprinkle with cinnamon and shaved chocolate. Chill.

Jolene Bontrager, Topeka, IN

Ice Cream

5 cups milk	¼ cup cornstarch
2 cups cane sugar	½ teaspoon sea salt
6 eggs, beaten	2 tablespoons vanilla
1 cup milk	2 cups Rich's topping

In saucepan, scald 5 cups milk with sugar. In mixing bowl, beat together eggs, 1 cup milk, cornstarch, and salt. Pour into scalded milk and bring to a boil. Boil over low for several minutes, stirring to prevent scorching. Add vanilla. Cool. (This part can be made a day before.) In bowl, beat Rich's topping to peaks. Blend into cold custard mixture. Freeze in ice cream freezer. Yield: 4 quarts.

Julia Troyer, Fredericksburg, OH

ICE CREAM DESSERT

1 (4 quart) bucket vanilla ice cream
1 (1 quart) bucket chocolate ice cream
2 (8 ounce) tubs whipped topping
1 package Oreo cookies, crushed

Soften ice cream for 15 minutes. In bowl, use electric mixer to mix vanilla ice cream with 8 ounces whipped topping. In separate bowl, mix chocolate ice cream with remaining 8 ounces whipped topping. Layer both mixtures into two 9x13-inch pans as follows: chocolate ice cream, half of cookie crumbs, vanilla ice cream, remaining cookie crumbs. Freeze. May also be prepared in individual cups.

Anna M. Byler, Clymer, PA

ICE CREAM SANDWICHES

3 eggs, divided*
½ cup powdered sugar
½ cup sugar
1 pint heavy cream, whipped
1 teaspoon vanilla
Graham crackers

Beat egg yolks and add sugars. Beat egg whites until stiff. Add egg whites and whipped cream to yolk mixture. Stir in vanilla. Spread mixture onto whole graham crackers. Freeze at around 0 degrees. Yield: 8 bars.

*Editor's note: use raw eggs with caution.

Mary Miller, Junction City, OH

DELICIOUS ICE CREAM

3 cups sugar
3 tablespoons flour
Pinch salt
8 cups milk, divided
4 eggs
1 (8 ounce) package cream
  cheese

1 teaspoon vanilla
3 cups chopped strawberries
  or raspberries
2 cups heavy cream or 1
  (14 ounce) can sweetened
  condensed milk

Boil together sugar, flour, salt, and 7 cups milk until thickened. In bowl, beat eggs with 1 cup milk. Add to cooked mixture. Heat to 160 degrees until mixture coats back of spoon. Stir in cream cheese until melted. Place pot in ice water to cool quickly. Stir for 2 minutes. Add vanilla. Cover with plastic wrap, pressing it down to seal air away from surface. Refrigerate several hours or overnight. Stir in berries and cream. Freeze in ice cream freezer.

Velma Schrock, Goshen, IN

CHOCOLATE DIP

1½ cups sugar
3 tablespoons butter
4 tablespoons cocoa powder

1 cup evaporated milk
1 teaspoon vanilla

In saucepan, boil together sugar, butter, cocoa powder, and milk for 7 minutes. Add vanilla. Serve warm over ice cream.

Lydiann Yoder, Andover, OH

AMISH WEDDINGS

by Wanda E. Brunstetter

The Amish wedding season often occurs in the fall, after the harvest is completed. However, in some areas, Amish weddings are held at other times throughout the year. The bride and groom both have two attendants, called *Newehockers* or *Newesitzers* (side sitters). Other helpers include the *Forgeher* (ushers), the waiters who serve tables during the meal afterward, the cooks, the helpers who set up tables, and the *Hostlers* (the boys who take care of the horses).

An Amish bride's dress is typically blue or purple and is made in the same style as the dresses Amish women wear to church. The bride and her attendants wear white capes and aprons over their dresses, as well as small white *kapps* (head coverings). Amish grooms wear black suits and white shirts. Some also wear black bow ties, which are seldom worn for regular church services.

Amish weddings are usually held in the bride's home, and the service, which is similar to a regular preaching service, begins early in the morning. There is no wedding music, ring exchange, or kiss, as there is in traditional "English" (non-Amish) weddings. The bride and groom receive a time of counseling while their guests sing a song. During the wedding service, scriptures are read, sermons are given, and prayers are said. The bride and groom then stand before the bishop, who asks them questions, similar to what the English do during their wedding vows. At the end of the service, the wedding meal is served to all the guests in attendance.

RECIPES FOR
FEEDING A CROWD

TIPS FOR FEEDING A CROWD

◆ Set up tables for the food. At the head of the tables, arrange trays/plates. Silverware and napkins are already placed on the tables where people will be seated to eat. Have the dishes of food arranged accordingly: hot dishes first, then salads, and last dessert. Put two serving spoons in each dish. Have the men file by on one side of the table and the ladies on the other (or however you prefer). Another idea is to have parents grouped with their children so they can both help the little ones fill their plates. After people have been seated, start serving drinks. Water can already be on the tables in pitchers.

Mrs. Ivan Yoder, Junction City, OH

◆ When planning a big gathering, just tell so many to bring a hot dish and so many to bring a cold dish. Then you will have a variety and plenty, and also cut down on the headache of how many you need of one kind.

Amanda Zehr, Spencerville, IN

Orange Punch

5 (46 ounce) cans pineapple
  juice
2 (46 ounce) cans water
3 (6 ounce) cans frozen orange
  juice concentrate
3 (6 ounce) cans frozen
  lemonade concentrate
3 (6 ounce) cans frozen
  limeade concentrate
¼ cup lemon juice
3 to 4 cups sugar
6 (2 liter) bottles lemon-lime
  soda

Combine first 7 ingredients; chill. Add soda just before serving. Yield: approximately 100 servings.

Fran Nissley, Campbellsville, KY

Wedding Fruit Mix

1 gallon fruit cocktail
1 gallon pineapple chunks
2 gallons sliced peaches
Pineapple juice
2½ cups clear-jel
1 package orange Kool-Aid
6 cups sugar
2 quarts green grapes
2 quarts red seedless grapes
12 kiwi
2 quarts apples, unpeeled
2 quarts fresh strawberries

Drain fruit cocktail, pineapple, and peaches. To the juice, add enough pineapple juice to make 1¾ gallons juice. In large pot, bring juice to a boil. Combine clear-jel and enough water to make a paste. Slowly add to boiling juice and cook until thickened and clear. Add Kool-Aid and sugar. On morning of wedding, cut grapes in half, slice kiwi crosswise, cut apples in chunks, and slice strawberries. Mix all fruits and pour sauce over all. Leftovers can be canned in water bath to preserve.

VARIATION: Add oranges, tangerines, or bananas. (Note: bananas cannot be canned.)

Serves approximately 100 people.

Irene Hershberger, McKenzie, TN

Broccoli Salad

11 large heads cauliflower
19 heads broccoli
10 pounds bacon, fried and crumbled

9 dozen hard-boiled eggs
8 pounds finely shredded cheese

Shred cauliflower, broccoli, and eggs. Put in very big bowl. Add bacon and cheese. Coat with dressing.

Dressing:

2 gallons Miracle Whip salad dressing
11 cups sugar

¼ scant cup salt
1 cup sour cream and onion powder

Mix all ingredients together.

Serves approximately 325 people.

Fran Nissley, Campbellsville, KY

Plate Salad

6 heads cauliflower
4 heads lettuce
6 heads cabbage
6 stalks celery
2 (1 pound) packages carrots, shredded

8 cups shredded cheese
2 quarts chopped ham
6 boxes Ritz crackers, crumbed

Chop up vegetables. Layer vegetables, in order given, on large cake plate. Mix sauce and pour over top. Layer cheese, ham, and cracker crumbs on top.

Sauce:

1 gallon mayonnaise or creamy salad dressing
6 cups ranch dressing
6 cups sugar

4 teaspoons sour cream and onion powder
Salt and pepper to taste

Blend ingredients well.

Serves approximately 280 people.

Sarah Hershberger, McKenzie, TN

Potato Salad

42 cups shredded cooked
    potatoes
42 eggs, boiled and shredded

7 cups chopped celery
5 cups chopped onion
    (optional)

Combine all ingredients and coat with dressing.

Dressing:

10½ cups Miracle Whip salad
    dressing
⅔ cup mustard

5½ cups sugar
⅞ cup vinegar
¼ cup + 2 teaspoons salt

Mix all together until smooth.

Serves approximately 150 people.

Fran Nissley, Campbellsville, KY

Chicken Stockpot Noodles

2 quarts chicken pieces
1½ quarts chicken broth
2½ gallons water
1¾ cups chicken soup base

5 pounds homemade noodles
4 cans cream of chicken soup
1 cup water
1½ cups butter, browned

In large stockpot, bring to a boil chicken, broth, 2½ gallons water, and soup base. Add noodles and cook 5 minutes. Mix cream of chicken soup with 1 cup water. Pour on top of noodle soup. Pour butter on top of that. Do not stir. Put lid on and let set for 1 hour before serving. Yield: 20 quarts to serve 80 people.

Katie Miller, Arthur, IL

Mixed Beans

15 pounds bacon or
   8 pounds ground beef
30 medium onions, chopped
4 gallons red kidney beans
4 gallons butter beans
4 gallons pork & beans

1 gallon bean of choice
   (pinto, black, navy, etc.)
8¾ quarts ketchup
¾ cup mustard
8 cups brown sugar

Fry bacon with onions. Drain. Combine with beans. Blend ketchup, mustard, and brown sugar. Pour over bean mixture. Divide into roasters. Bake at 350 degrees for 2 hours.

Serves approximately 450 people.

Fran Nissley, Campbellsville, KY

Mashed Potatoes

6 quarts potatoes, cooked
Milk

1 (8 ounce) package cream
   cheese
1 cup sour cream

Mash potatoes, making them fairly thin with added milk. Add cream cheese and sour cream. Refrigerate no longer than 2 days. (Also freezes well.) Heat slowly in oven.

We use this recipe for church carry-ins or benefit dinners.

Mrs. Ervin (Susan) Byler, Crab Orchard, KY

Chicken Gravy

1½ cups butter
2 cups flour
2 quarts chicken broth

1 tablespoon chicken base
1 teaspoon seasoned salt
Pepper

Brown butter in large pan or skillet. Add flour, stirring to lightly brown. Add broth, stirring as it thickens. Thin with a little water if needed. Sprinkle with chicken base, seasoned salt, and pepper, stirring in.

Serves approximately 30 people.

Mrs. John D. Miller, Millersburg, OH

Amish Dressing

10 loaves bread, toasted and cubed
3 quarts shredded potatoes
2 quarts chopped celery, cooked
1 quart shredded carrots
1 pint chopped onion
1½ cups diced celery leaves
5 quarts chicken broth or 3 quarts broth + 2 quarts cooked chicken
2 pounds butter
4 ounces soup base
6 dozen eggs
Salt and pepper to taste
3 to 4 quarts milk

Divide bread, potatoes, celery, carrots, onion, and celery leaves in 3 large roasters (or 4 small roasters). Heat chicken broth, butter, and soup base. Pour over bread and vegetables. Beat eggs; add salt and pepper and milk. Pour over all. Bake at 350 degrees for 1 hour.

Serves approximately 300 people.

Mrs. Levi J. Stutzman, West Salem, OH

Chicken and Dressing

6 quarts chopped celery
3 quarts chopped onion
6 pounds butter, melted
1½ quarts cubed cooked potatoes
1 quart canned carrots
3 gallons chicken broth
6 dozen eggs, beaten
6 quarts milk
18 (1.5 pound) loaves bread, crumbled
1½ gallons shredded cooked chicken
⅓ cup salt
4 teaspoons pepper
4 teaspoons ground sage

Cook celery and onion in some of the butter. (If you don't have canned carrots, they can also be cooked ahead of time.) Mix all ingredients together and put into roasters. Bake at 350 degrees for 3 hours.

Serves approximately 300 people.

Fran Nissley, Campbellsville, KY

Ranch Potato Casserole

3 pounds ground beef, browned
2 cans cream of mushroom soup
1 gallon diced cooked potatoes

2 cups sour cream
2 cups ranch dressing
1 pound bacon, fried and crumbled
Shredded cheese

Mix beef with soup. In large roaster, layer beef mixture, then potatoes. Blend sour cream and ranch dressing and pour over potatoes. Cover with bacon. Bake at 350 degrees for 45 to 60 minutes until hot. Sprinkle with cheese and allow to melt. Yield: 35 servings.

Verna Stutzman, Navarre, OH

Reunion Potatoes

9 pounds potatoes
3 cans cream of mushroom soup
1 can cream of celery soup
1 (2 pound) box Velveeta cheese
1 cup butter

Dash pepper
3 cups milk
1 cup mayonnaise or creamy salad dressing
4 teaspoons seasoned salt
¾ cup chopped onion
1 teaspoon salt

Boil potatoes with a little salt. (Boil in skins the day before, and peel and dice right before ready to prepare.) In saucepan, mix remaining ingredients and heat until butter and cheese are melted. Put potatoes in roaster and pour sauce over top. Bake at 350 degrees for 1 hour.

Serves 20 to 25 people.

Irene Hershberger, McKenzie, TN

Noodle Casserole for Roaster

3 packages noodles
2 pounds Velveeta cheese
5 pounds ground beef

3 large cans cream of chicken soup
½ to ¾ soup can full of milk

Cook and drain noodles. Add cheese and let melt. Fry ground beef until done. Mix in soup and milk. In large roaster, stir together cheesy noodles and beef mixture. Bake at 350 degrees for 1 hour.

Mrs. Levi J. Stutzman, West Salem, OH

Wedding Chicken

40 pounds chicken
½ cup salt
¼ cup brown sugar
1 gallon water

12 eggs, beaten
4 cups milk
2 cups salad dressing

Fill 5-gallon pail with chicken pieces. Combine salt, brown sugar, and water. Pour over chicken, cover, and refrigerate overnight. Next day, drain off liquid. Beat eggs, milk, and salad dressing. Dip chicken in egg mixture then roll in crumb coating. Place on cookie sheets. Bake at 375 to 400 degrees for about 1 hour. Move to roasters, covered, and bake at 350 degrees for 60 to 90 minutes until tender (or it reaches 165 degrees near the bone).

Crumb Coating:

4 boxes crackers, crumbed fine
1 box cornflake cereal
8 cups flour

1 cup seasoned salt
1 teaspoon garlic powder
4 ounces paprika

Mix all and keep in airtight container until ready to use.

This recipe is used often at weddings, including at our own.

Jonas and Sarah Gingerich, Junction City, OH

Meat Loaf

36 pounds ground beef
9 cups quick oats
9 cups finely crushed
    crackers
4 cups finely chopped onion
4 tablespoons salt

3 teaspoons pepper
2 dozen eggs
2½ quarts milk
1 quart beef broth
1 quart tomato juice

Combine all and mix well. Pack firmly into pans or roasters. Bake at 350 to 375 degrees for 4 hours or until well done in center. Cover with sauce and bake an additional 10 to 15 minutes.

Sauce:

8⅔ cups ketchup
2 cups mustard

3 cups brown sugar

Mix together.

Serves approximately 200 people.

Elizabeth N. Borntrager, Clark, MO

Wedding Steak

45 pounds ground beef or turkey
30 cups saltine cracker crumbs
30 cups milk
15 tablespoons salt

2½ cups minced onion
5 teaspoons pepper
5 cans cream of mushroom soup
4 cans milk
1 box Velveeta cheese

Mix beef, cracker crumbs, 30 cups milk, salt, onion, and pepper and form into patties. Brown patties on both sides. In pot, heat together soup, 4 cans milk, and cheese until cheese melts. Arrange patties in 5 roasters and pour sauce over all. Bake at 350 degrees for 1 hour or until heated through.

Serves approximately 250 people.

Irene Hershberger, McKenzie, TN

Pulled Pork

15-to-20-pound Boston butt pork roast

Place in large slow cooker, fat side up. Do not add liquid. Cook on high for 3 to 4 hours. Turn down to low for an additional 7 hours. Remove from slow cooker and debone meat. Pull meat apart to shred. Cool meat and store in refrigerator up to 5 days. Heat again in slow cooker or oven. Serve on sandwich buns with sauce.

Sauce:

2 cups water
2 cups vinegar
2¾ cups ketchup
½ cup sugar
1 tablespoon red pepper flakes
2 tablespoons pepper
2 teaspoons celery seed

2 teaspoons dry mustard
1½ teaspoons salt
1½ teaspoons poultry seasoning
1½ teaspoons rubbed sage
8 ounces A.1. sauce
5 ounces Heinz 57 sauce

Combine all ingredients in large saucepan, bring to a boil and simmer 10 minutes. Store in bottles in refrigerator. Serve with pulled pork.

Serves approximately 75 people.

Makes an excellent picnic main dish. Serve sandwiches with coleslaw, picnic eggs, and potato chips.

Kathryn Troyer, Rutherford, TN

Big Batch Chocolate Chip Cookies

10 cups shortening
10 cups sugar
10 cups brown sugar
20 eggs
2½ cups hot water

8 teaspoons vanilla
10 teaspoons baking soda
8 teaspoons salt
32 cups flour
8 cups chocolate chips

Mix all together. Bake at 350 degrees for 9 to 12 minutes. Yield: approximately 30 dozen.

Mrs. Sarah Gingerich, Howard, OH

Index of Contributors

Laura Miller, Mount Vernon, OH 22, 57, 112

Liz Miller, Decatur, IN 148

Lizzie Miller, Andover, OH 51

Lydia Miller, Loudonville, OH 70, 113

Mary Miller, Junction City, OH 169, 191

Rachel D. Miller, Millersburg, OH 126

Ruby Miller, Auburn, KY 186

Mrs. John H. Mullet, Cass City, MI 92, 147

Fran Nissley, Campbellsville, KY 197, 198, 199, 201, 202

Esther M. Peachey, Flemingsburg, KY 73, 90, 107

Phebe Peight, McVeytown, PA 38, 56, 100, 130, 142

Anita Lorraine Petersheim, Fredericktown, OH 48, 105, 158, 185

Kari Danette Petersheim, Fredericktown, OH 15, 73, 87

Martha Petersheim, Junction City, OH 135, 147, 151

Mattie Petersheim, Junction City, OH 66, 84, 166, 170

Mary Joyce Petersheim, Fredericktown, OH 61

Rosanna Petersheim, Mifflin, PA 26

Miriam Raber, Flat Rock, IL 11, 183

Doris Schlabach, Goshen, IN 25

Mrs. Robert (Shirley) Schlabach, Crofton, KY 182

Mrs. Emanuel Schmidt, Carlisle, KY 133

Katie Schmidt, Carlisle, KY 36

Mrs. Martin A. Schmidt, Carlisle, KY 98

Rebecca Schmidt, Carlisle, KY 176

Mrs. Lavern Schrock, Marion, MI 141, 175

Velma Schrock, Goshen, IN 32, 76, 129, 146, 192

Ann Schwartz, Salem, IN 89

Emma Schwartz, Berne, IN 180

Esther Schwartz, Harrisville, PA 51, 95

Ida R. Schwartz, Salem, IN 161, 165

Laura R. Schwartz, Bryant, IN 104

Lizzie Schwartz, Berne, IN 150, 176, 179

Rosina Schwartz, Salem, IN 78

Mrs. Samuel J. Schwartz, Bryant, IN 92, 123, 168

Susan R. Schwartz, Bryant, IN 124

Verena N. Schwartz, Scottsburg, IN 40, 42

Elizabeth Shetler, Brinkhaven, OH 11, 134

Mrs. Alfred (Barbara) Stutzman, Danville, OH 40

Mrs. Levi J. Stutzman, West Salem, OH 74, 106, 172, 202, 204

Verna Stutzman, Navarre, OH 53, 86, 99, 203

Julia Troyer, Fredericksburg, OH 38, 83, 122, 190

Kathryn Troyer, Rutherford, TN 14, 26, 47, 50, 59, 121, 148, 178, 184, 207

Mary Ellen Wengerd, Campbellsville, KY 47, 68, 85, 108, 179

Mrs. Albert (Ruth) Yoder, Stanwood, MI 67

Anna M. Yoder, Mercer, MO 66, 129

B. Saloma D. Yoder, Mercer, MO 78, 90, 132

Doretta Yoder, Topeka, IN 17

Ella Arlene Yoder, Arcola, IL 164

Erma Yoder, Middlefield, OH 15

Iva Yoder, Goshen, IN 35, 169

Mrs. Ivan Yoder, Junction City, OH 175, 188, 196

Lydiann Yoder, Andover, OH 29, 115, 180, 192

Mrs. Orley (Dianna) Yoder, Goshen, IN 58, 79

Amanda Zehr, Spencerville, IN 66, 196

Emma Zook, Navarre, OH 51

Index of Recipes by Section

RECIPES FOR SIDE DISHES

RECIPES FOR MAIN DISHES

RECIPES FOR DESSERTS

Cakes

Bars and Cookies

Pies

Puddings

Other Desserts

RECIPES FOR FEEDING A CROWD

Index of Recipes by Key Ingredients